Positive Approaches to
Learning Disability

A workbook to support the Certificates in Working with People who have Learning Disabilities

A L I C E   B R A D L E Y

Acknowledgements

The assistance of the following people is gratefully acknowledged:

- all members of the Quality Action Group, Stirling, for generously allowing the use of their premises for meetings with the Advisory and Support Group
- Steve McKee, in particular, for facilitating our meetings
- Yvonne Bradley, of Falkirk College of Further and Higher Education, for her help and liaison activities
- most especially, Andrew Forbes, Anne Young, David Kinloch, Idem Lewis, Karen Patrick and Stuart Adams for their valuable contributions to this workbook.

British Library Cataloguing in Publication Data

A CIP record for this book is available from the Public Library

ISBN 1 904082 01 7

© 2002 BILD Publications

BILD Publications is the publishing office of:
British Institute of Learning Disabilities
Campion House
Green Street
Kidderminster
Worcestershire DY10 1JL

Telephone: 01562 723010
Fax: 01562 723029
E-mail: enquiries@bild.org.uk
Website: www.bild.org.uk

Please contact BILD for a free publications catalogue listing BILD books, training materials and journals.

BILD publications are distributed worldwide by:
Plymbridge Distributors
Plymbridge House
Estover Road
Plymouth
United Kingdom
PL6 7PZ

Telephone: 01752 202301
Fax: 01752 202333

Positive Approaches to Learning Disability

Contents

How the cause of a learning disability may affect society's attitude

Accessing literature and information to write a report

Writing a report on the causation of a learning disability in relation to
a service user

Introduction

The danger of expectations

Knowing about the effects of a syndrome or condition

Researching information and producing a report on the possible effects of a
syndrome or condition

The role of support and information groups

Introduction

The social construction of disability

The implications of the social construction of disability for people with
learning disabilities

The disabling effects of society's response to learning disability

Comments on the disabling effects of society's response from the
Advisory and Support Group

Introduction

Introduction

Welcome to *Positive Approaches to Learning Disability*. This is a study workbook designed to provide the essential information for people undertaking the mandatory units of the Level 2 and Level 3 *Certificates in Working with People who have Learning Disabilities*. The workbook covers all of the learning outcomes for the level 2 unit 008 Understand Learning Disability and the level 3 unit 104 Understand Approaches to Learning Disability.

This workbook is one of a series of eight covering all of the Mandatory units, designed for staff in services supporting people with a learning disability. Units can be studied on their own or in groups or clusters. Each workbook covers all of the learning outcomes for the level 2 and 3 unit. The Mandatory series includes:

- Positive Approaches to Communication
- Positive Approaches to Handling Information
- Positive Approaches to Understanding and Managing Risk
- Positive Approaches to Learning Disability
- Positive Approaches to Protecting from Abuse
- Positive Approaches to Anti-Oppressive Practice
- Positive Approaches to Assessing Care Planning
- Positive Approaches to Reviewing Care Plans.

The last two units on care planning are mandatory units for the level 3 *Certificate in Working with People who have Learning Disabilities* and in the optional group A for the Level 2 qualification.

It is possible to use this workbook:

- for your own personal study
- as part of an accredited learning programme, with a certificate to show what you have successfully learned (see page 7).
- to support in-house training or mentoring sessions.

Likely users

This workbook is aimed at:

- staff who have completed their induction and foundation units and are taking further units from the Level 2 or Level 3 Certificates
- more experienced staff working with people with a learning disability, who want to extend their skills and knowledge

- managers with responsibilities for staff supervision
- training managers in services for people with learning disabilities.

Staff members

This workbook will help you with your studies towards one of the mandatory units from the *Certificates in Working with People who have Learning Disabilities*. The book covers all of the learning outcomes for the unit. You can use the book as part of a distance learning course, to support in house training sessions or as part of supervision you may be receiving from a colleague or mentor. In addition to undertaking a programme of learning you will also need to complete assessment tasks to provide evidence of your learning. Your assessment can be arranged by your centre or BILD can assist with assessment of your work. For further information refer to the resources section at the end of this workbook.

Managers with responsibilities for staff supervision

This workbook provides information and activities that you may find helpful in supporting staff in your service. It will be a useful resource in supervision sessions and should also be helpful for staff mentoring employees.

Training managers

If staff wish to use the learning they have completed in this workbook for accreditation towards the certificate, they need to be registered with one of the awarding bodies and studying on a recognised programme of study. They will also need to complete a portfolio of work for assessment. Further information on this can be obtained from BILD or the awarding bodies (see the resources section at the back of this workbook).

This workbook will be a useful resource for training managers planning and delivering units from the *Certificates in Working with People who have Learning Disabilities*. It can also be given to individual members of staff to:

- supplement training sessions
- consolidate learning
- assist learners in providing a portfolio of evidence, particularly for those seeking accreditation for their learning.

Relationship to other care qualifications

S/NVQ qualifications in care

Scottish/National Vocational Qualifications (S/NVQs) in Care and the level 2 and level 3 *Certificates in Working with People who have Learning Disabilities* are closely related qualifications. S/NVQs are related to National Occupational Standards and assess worker competence. The *Certificates* are

Vocationally Related Qualifications (VRQs). These are a relatively new type of qualification that assess a learner's knowledge and some skills, but do not assess workplace competence. VRQs can provide a structured way for learners to gain the required underpinning knowledge towards an S/NVQ. For further information on the relationship between S/NVQs and the *Certificates in Working with People who have Learning Disabilities*, go to the Learning Disabilities Awards Framework website at www.ldaf.org.uk.

Each unit from the two Certificates has been mapped to S/NVQ competences and can therefore be used to help learners acquire some of the underpinning knowledge towards an S/NVQ. Full details of the mapping for this unit can be obtained from the LDAF website www.ldaf.org.uk, from the Scheme Handbook for the Certificates or from the BILD assessment booklet for this unit.

Accreditation for your study

If you wish to receive accreditation for your study from this workbook, you will need to study on a programme provided by an organisation recognised by one of the awarding bodies (City and Guilds Affinity and National Open College Network) for the *Certificates in Working with People who have Learning Disabilities*.

BILD is one of the organisations recognised by the two awarding bodies – the City and Guilds and the National Open College Network. For more information about the BILD Certificates Programme, which provides in-house training, distance learning and supports satellite centres, please contact the Learning Services Administrator on 01562 723010.

Confidentiality and consent

An important aim of this workbook is to encourage you to relate what you are learning to your work situation. As part of this you will need to reflect on the way you work with people with a learning disability.

Before involving people with learning disabilities in any activities from this workbook, you need to make sure they understand what you are doing and obtain their consent. Discuss this with your line manager before going ahead. A few activities are based on discussions or observations of colleagues or people with learning disabilities; when you write these up you need to be aware of the need for confidentiality. Never refer to anyone by their real name. Instead, always use an alias (a false name) or an initial to identify the person. Discuss your organisation's confidentiality policy with your line manager before completing any of the activities.

Labels and terms

There has been a great deal of debate about how to describe people with learning disabilities. Ideally we should call everyone by their names, since the most important thing to recognise is that each person is an individual, with a different personality, characteristics, strengths and failings. However, there are times when labels, no matter how much we dislike them, are used for all of us – student, parent, teenager, claimant, senior citizen, patient. Some labels carry negative connotations, some positive.

Throughout this workbook I use the term *learning disability*, which is the most commonly used term in health and social care settings. The terms 'mental handicap' and the American term 'mental retardation' are considered inappropriate and people with learning disabilities find them unacceptable. The term *people with learning difficulties* is preferred by the organisation People First which is run by people with learning disabilities. This term is also used in some education settings.

As you go through the workbook you will find I sometimes use the term *service user* to refer to people with learning disabilities, as they are the users of the service you work for. The people with learning disabilities, who acted as an Advisory and Support Group for all of the workbooks in this series, dislike the term 'service user'. This is largely because of its connotations of dependence and the fact that it does not reflect their participation as equal partners and, in some cases, as managers of services. They also prefer the term 'disabled person' to 'person with a learning disability', since this highlights the fact that it is society which disables people because of the way it is constructed. However, we were unable to find a 'label' which satisfied ourselves. I have decided, therefore, to continue to use the terms which are most commonly used at present. In doing this, I acknowledge their limitations.

If you are studying this workbook, you're likely to be a paid member of staff, so I've generally used the terms *workers* or *practitioners*. However, much of the workbook content also applies if you are a volunteer or family carer.

I have also tried to avoid gender bias by using *he* or *she* alternately, except where this becomes clumsy or when I am referring to a particular person.

I use the word *service* to refer to your workplace situation, whether it is residential, day provision, based in the community or elsewhere. The word *organisation* refers to the agency that runs your service. Any other terms that may not be clear are explained as they arise.

The Advisory and Support Group

A group of six people with learning disabilities contributed to this workbook as an Advisory and Support Group (referred to throughout the workbook as the A&S Group). Five of them were from the Quality Action Group in Stirling, a group run by people with learning disabilities. The sixth was from Glasgow and on committees too numerous to mention, as he himself says.

We met approximately every two weeks for a period of six months, sometimes in the evening and sometimes during the day, depending on the commitments of all of us. During our meetings, we discussed the issues that are the focus of this workbook and the others in the series. Needless to say, we never had enough time to finish our discussions. The opinions and experiences of this group appear in different places throughout the workbook.

The people in the A&S Group introduce themselves below.

Anne Young

'I'm Anne Young. I'm the chairperson of the Quality Action Group. I make sure the agenda's ready for meetings and that and make sure everybody's there in a decent time – some people are late and say 'I'm sorry I'm late' and I say 'That's OK – just make sure it doesn't happen again' – only joking! I tell them to get there on time. And I'm working at the café and I do get paid, doing the tables and the dishes. Every Saturday. The rest of the week I'm at college as well and do something with key workers as well, they're supporting me to do my shopping and that. I'm doing how to look for jobs and that – community studies. In my spare time I go to the pub, have a drink and that, and I talk. I live in a flat by myself and have 24-hour support – I'm getting there – I like it. My message to key workers: have a look at the book, and hopefully like it, what we've done. Try to understand what we're looking for.'

Karen Patrick

'I'm Karen Patrick, I'm the vice-treasurer of the Quality Action Group. I do the finance and the cash books – writing up cheques, get the finance right. I'm in a lot of meetings just now – me and Idem are trustees for the Scottish Consortium for Learning Disabilities – we don't like the word 'centre', that's why it's called 'consortium'. We go to trustee meetings and board meetings – interviewing people for the consortium, the admin and the director. I live beside Anne in a flat. I share with Cheryl. I also go to college. I only go on a Thursday. But I'm hoping to do more next year. I'm doing Home Economics.

I do a volunteering job – I go every Monday – helping out in Letts café. I'm busy most of the year. I've got some spare time but not a lot.'

Idem Lewis

'Hello, my name is Idem Lewis. I live in Glasgow. I'm on a lot of committees – too many to mention. I'm in Key Housing, at Head Office at various times every week, doing meetings, organising meetings, organising speeches. I'm also on the board of trustees at the Scottish Consortium for Learning Disabilities. I'm an anti-racist activist at the Trade Unions, also for Disability Rights in Scotland; I'm also vice-chair of Learning Disability Alliance, Scotland and I'm the user chair on the user-carer group. I'm also an anti-poverty campaigner at night. So I'm a bit busy sometimes. I also like to visit friends and watching TV is my hobby. I play basketball on a Saturday – I played at Special Olympics. I stay in a top floor flat in Glasgow.

I was involved in the Learning Disabilities Review. The Scottish Executive came to attend the Advisory Group at Key Housing Head Office. We had a workshop about what matters most and we said to the Advisory Group what we want – accessible transport etc, and we made it into a report, "The Same As You?" – so I've been to meetings and seminars and made one or two speeches.'

David Kinloch

'Hello, my name is David. I'm the secretary of the Quality Action Group. Also I have a volunteer job working at Animal Welfare – I work two days a week in the van, sometimes I work at nights as well, because sometimes I get called out at night time if there's any animals being neglected or abused by owners. I've got three pets of my own which I took on from the animal rescue centre. I'm also a member of the Disabled Alliance Group; also I'm a volunteer team leader in the youth club up in Bannockburn. And my spare time is with friends – I don't go to the pub – well, I don't go to the pub a lot – I just really go for the odd drink and that, but mostly I just sit and relax and look after my pets. That's what I do. And I help my mother as well, because usually I go up on a weekend and see if she's needing any shopping or that, and on a Sunday I go up and see her at the day centre where she works.

I've got my own house, it's a council house. I'm my own tenant. I've got a big white rabbit and two guinea pigs, which I love. The rabbit's called Whitey and the guinea pig that's got the ears sticking up is called Barney, and I've got another one called Ginger who's an orangey colour, with white bands.

I made a speech to the Scottish Executive. That was about hospital closure. That was the launch of Disabled Alliance. Some of us – there was quite a lot of folk there – and after that the group took off. I'm still going to the Disabled Alliance meetings, but not all the time because sometimes they've got a meeting on a Saturday and I'm working, so it's quite hard to get up because at the moment I don't have anybody to cover for me. So if I want to take a couple of days I have to find someone to cover for me.'

Andrew Forbes

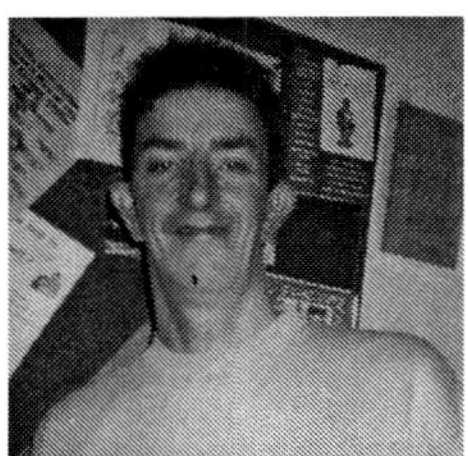

'My name's Andrew. I'm the vice-secretary [of the Quality Action Group]. I help with the minutes, make sure the treasurer's minutes are on time and I also do minutes for the management committee. Also I'm on the general council for the Alpha Centre (leisure centre) – I made history by becoming the first disability person there. The things I like to do – I walk my dog, I'm an amateur fossil collector, I'm also a wee bit of a counsellor – listening to other people's worries, advise them. I live on my own, my sister's just a stone's throw away, me and my dog live together in the house – it's a council house.

I hope you find this book very interesting and I hope you enjoy the book.'

Stuart Adams

'My name is Stuart Adams. I'm the vice-chairperson of the Quality Action Group. I am also a committee member of the Central TAG group (Tenants Advisory Group). I go to college on a Wednesday and a Friday. On the Wednesday first thing, I do Exploring Europe, and in the afternoon it is Surfing the Internet. On a Friday all day it's Access to Mainstream. All morning and afternoon. I live in a council house which is sub-let on to Key, in Larbert Cross, in the main street. I'm on the committee of the Campaigning Group for Learning Disabilities. It's a Key Housing campaign. Me and Idem's on that. Trying to get people's attitudes changed so that, like, there was something to do with a poster for buses that people understand – the Enable poster – getting it out into the community. I was also on the Learning Disabilities Review, trying to get people's ideas and thoughts so that we can get out to people who do not know how we feel.'

I am extremely grateful to all of the people in this group for their input. I really enjoyed working with them. I've also included some information about myself here.

Alice Bradley

My name is Alice Bradley and I live in Hamilton, near Glasgow. I've recently ventured into self-employment as a freelance trainer, having been employed in organisations all my working life. I've also recently become an Open University tutor. I've been working with children and adults with learning disabilities, and their families, for a very long time, both in a paid and voluntary capacity. My background is in education and I've worked in schools, higher education and adult services. I've lived and worked in Scotland, England, Wales, Canada and Thailand. I've also been involved in training and development projects in several countries in Asia and Africa. It's been great working with Anne, Karen, Andrew, David, Idem and Stuart of the Advisory and Support Group and I hope we'll have the chance to work together again.

How to use these materials

We all vary in how we study and in our learning patterns. Some people prefer to study in short bursts, spreading their learning over a long period. Others prefer more sustained periods of concentration. Some of us like to study early in the day; others don't start until later in the evening. No one way of studying is better than another. What matters is finding the way that suits you.

Whatever your preference, there are certain things you can do to make studying easier.

- Keep a pen or pencil with you while reading this workbook. Write comments in the margins or underline bits you find interesting or thought-provoking.
- Try to find a place for study where you will be undisturbed, and where you can leave your work safely.
- Plan a timetable that allows you to set aside time to study.
- Break the unit down into manageable chunks that you know you can complete in a set time.
- Keep your written work and any information you collect in a loose-leaf ringbinder.
- Discuss your study regularly with your line manager and colleagues. This will help you to think about how you can use the ideas from this workbook in your day-to-day support of people with learning disabilities.

These materials are interactive. As well as reading them, you will also need to:

- think about things
- give your own ideas and opinions

- talk to colleagues
- try out some activities.

There are different kinds of activities and you will need a pen and paper for some of them.

Unless learning is applied to your work, it is not very useful. So, throughout the workbook, summary 'Key points' bring together the key ideas in the workbook and help you to put them into practice.

How this workbook is organised

The focus of this workbook is on understanding society's view of, and response to, people with learning disabilities. As people who work with those who have learning disabilities, we all have a responsibility to support them in their struggle for equal rights. This workbook will give you the opportunity to think about the changes that have taken place in society over recent years. While there is an exploration of the effects of various conditions, the focus is very much on the person rather than the disability.

There are five sections in this workbook:

1 Human growth and development

This section is concerned with the process of development, the importance of the physical and social environment on the developing child and the way in which learning disability affects individuals.

2 Changes in understanding about learning disabilities

Over recent years there have been substantial changes in our knowledge and understanding of learning disabilities. These are explored in section two.

3 The person, not the disability

'People first' has become a well recognised slogan and is what we focus on in this section, not denying the disability, but regarding it as a secondary consideration to the person, him or herself.

4 Expectations, information and experiences

Section four warns about the danger of limiting your expectations of people with learning disabilities, or of having particular expectations based on your awareness of their syndrome or condition. In this section we also discuss the ways in which information about a particular syndrome or condition might be useful in helping you provide the right kind of support to an individual, or avoid potentially harmful situations.

5 The disabling effects of society's response to learning disabilities

In the final section , we examine the way in which society's perceptions of, and behaviour towards, people with learning disabilities disables them much more than their impairment.

I suggest you do the workbook activities as you work through the materials. You'll also find workplace activities at the end of each section. Doing these activities will help you to absorb the information and improve your work as a practitioner.

Important documents

At certain places in the workbook you will come across extracts from two very important documents:

Department of Health (2001) *Valuing People: A New Strategy for Learning Disability for the 21st Century*, London: Department of Health, the White Paper for England which, in the words of the Prime Minister:

'*...sets out this Government's commitment to improving the life chances of people with learning disabilities*'. (p.1)

Scottish Executive (2000) *The Same As You? A Review of Services for People with Learning Disabilities*, Edinburgh: Scottish Executive, to which the people in the A&S Group contributed, which, in the words of the Deputy Minister for Community Care:

'*... began by looking at services, especially in social and health care, and their relationship with education, housing, employment and other areas. However, its focus changed to include people's lifestyles. That is what matters. Services are there to support people in their daily lives.*' (p.1)

To download a PDF version of these documents from the internet, the addresses are as follows:

Valuing People – www.archive.official-documents.co.uk/document/cm50/5086/5086.pdf

The Same as You? – www.scotland.gov.uk/library3/social/tsay.pdf.

Good luck with your studying and enjoy the workbook!

Section 1:
Human growth and development

Human growth and development

Introduction

If you have young children, or have close relatives with young children, you'll be aware of how quickly they change from one day to the next. We now know that the first three years of a child's life is a period of growth and development unlike any other. A knowledge of human growth and development is helpful in understanding why and how learning disability occurs, which is why I explore the following topics in this first section:

- milestones in human growth and development
- the effects of social and physical environment on individual growth and development
- how learning disability affects different people
- how a knowledge of human growth and development relates to your work.

Milestones in growth and development

Babies develop at an amazing rate, although probably not as rapidly as the cartoon suggests! One day the infant is lying in his cot, dependent on adults for everything. Then, in a remarkably short space of time, he's climbing on tables, throwing his food around and generally making a strong impression on his environment!

The baby's brain is not fully developed at birth, but undergoes dramatic changes in the first three years of life. It produces billions of new cells and makes a multitude of connections between these cells. As the brain develops and new connections are made, so the child's physical, cognitive (intellectual), social and emotional development progresses and he becomes suitably equipped to function effectively within his environment.

To help us understand human growth and development more easily, we generally think of it in terms of the **developmental areas** mentioned above:

- physical development
- cognitive development
- social and emotional development.

All these areas of development are inter-related. But not all develop at the same rate. For example, the baby's thinking skills (cognitive) might be in advance of movement abilities (physical), as in the example of 4-month-old Emma.

Example

Emma, 4 months old, is lying on a blanket on the living room floor. She spies a favourite toy several yards away and tries to reach for it, but is too far away. She tries to move towards it but can't, as she hasn't yet got the motor skills to do so. She screams until her father comes, he realises finally what she wants and gives the toy to her.

In which of the developmental areas outlined above (physical, cognitive, social and emotional) would you say Emma's skills are in advance of another? Note your ideas down here.

If Emma were a little older she'd be able to pull herself forward or roll over to get the toy. But, although she can't get to the toy herself, she knows how to make things happen in the way she wants – she attracts attention by screaming until her father guesses what she wants and gets it for her. This is a good example of cognitive (intellectual) development being in advance of motor (physical) development.

Each area of development is affected by the other and determines what is and is not possible for the child. For example, the 2-year-old (the 'terrible twos') wants to be independent and make her own decisions, but her level of development in *all* areas determines what she is capable of doing. It may be alright for her to choose what to have for breakfast or what toys she wants to play with, but crossing the road independently or walking along by herself in a busy shopping area cannot be permitted. She knows what she wants to do – as evidenced by the number of mothers we see hanging on to crying children who want to walk on their own – and can cope with it *physically*, but is not yet equipped *cognitively* to understand danger, look for cars and take evasive action if need be.

No two children develop at the same rate. Physical development might be slower than emotional and social development in some and faster in others, for example. Some children walk at 9 months, most around 12 to 14 months, and others later. There's a wide age range for every aspect of development, which is why you might hear a doctor or health visitor say that a child is 'within the normal range'. Even brothers and sisters brought up in the same family differ in their rate of development, as you may know from your own experience.

Milestones

Some aspects of development are more significant than others. These are often referred to as **milestones** in a child's development, as they indicate to us how development is progressing. It's a concept you're probably familiar with and is one of the things a health visitor checks when children have their age-related assessments.

Physical development

Physical development occurs as a result of a combination of *maturation* and *development*. In other words, the child's body continues to increase in size, weight and muscular capacity and his brain goes on making new cells and new connections. At birth, the areas of the brain that control movement are not yet well developed. These areas develop in a head-to-toe sequence. Brain areas controlling head and neck muscles mature before those controlling arm and trunk muscles which, in turn, mature earlier than those controlling the legs.

At the same time, the child's small muscles are also developing. Small and large muscles begin working together. When talking about physical development, two areas of motor development are usually referred to – **gross motor development** (large muscle movements) and **fine motor development** (small muscle movements). The two lots of muscles working together involve **motor coordination**.

Major milestones in gross motor development

Major gross motor milestones include:

- head control – when the child is able to hold her head erect by herself, without it flopping, at around 3 months
- sitting unaided, without requiring any props or assistance, at around 6 to 8 months
- crawling happens around 9 months – not all children crawl; some go from pulling themselves up to walking
- walking by themselves, usually around 12 to 15 months.

It is important to remember that there is wide variation in the ages at which these milestones occur with different children. Personality and motivation can also play a part. For example, children who are outgoing, lively and energetic might be more inclined to move around more than children who are quieter in nature and who are quite happy to stay in one spot for a long time.

Other milestones, which come later and are helpful in understanding child development, but which are not as significant as those above, include:

- walking up stairs
- running
- jumping off things
- standing on one foot.

All milestones make certain things possible for the child. A group of children of the same age, left to their own devices, will do roughly the same things. Take crawling, for example. Before the child can crawl, she is more or less restricted to her immediate environment. But, once she learns to crawl, she can interact more extensively with the environment. All sorts of new adventures become possible. The kitchen's no longer tidy, the pots and pans don't stay in the cupboard and everything has to be moved out of reach – until she begins to climb (one reason why manufacturers make a lot of money from childproof locks and handles!).

Major milestones in fine motor development
Just as there are milestones in gross motor development, so there are in fine motor development. The major ones are:

- reaches out towards an object or person, at around 3 to 4 months
- grasps an object with the whole hand (palmar grasp), at about 4 months
- manipulates small objects, at around 5 months
- grasps an object between finger and thumb (pincer grasp), at around 11 months
- develops a preference for right or left hand, at around 13 months.

You can see how the development of fine motor skills, combined with that of gross motor skills, makes more and more activities available to the child. Toy manufacturers know this well, so toys on sale for newborn babies are brightly coloured objects that move in the wind, whereas toys for older children include objects they can touch, bang, throw and get a result from.

Vision
The development of vision is a crucial part of physical development. At birth, the baby cannot see very well. Distant objects are out of focus and each eye works independently. Initially he sleeps a lot, opening his eyes for short

periods. He responds most to bright light and movement. He doesn't yet have control of his eye movements, so these are jerky and uncoordinated at first. However, the visual part of his brain is the most active at this age. By the time he is about 7 months, his vision will be almost the same as an adult's.

The significant milestones in visual development are:

- being able to see objects at a distance
- seeing colour
- tracking movement
- the development of depth perception
- the coordination of both eyes, so that they work together.

If you look closely at the milestones for both gross and fine motor development, you will see that many of them involve not only motor movements, but also vision. This leads us on to another important area of physical development – the coordination of motor skills and vision. You will probably be familiar with the term 'hand-eye coordination', used to refer to the coordination of fine motor movements and vision.

Activity 1: Visual motor coordination

Read through the milestones under gross motor development and fine motor development again and you will see that many of them require the coordination of motor and visual skills.

List below the ones that require both visual and motor skills.

....

....

....

....

....

Comment
Did you include:

- *gross motor – crawling, walking, running, jumping off things*
- *fine motor – reaching out towards an object or person, grasping an object with the whole hand (palmar grasp), grasping an object between finger and thumb (pincer grasp)?*

Hand-eye coordination is vitally important for the developing child and, indeed, throughout life. Think about what is involved in such everyday activities as driving, crossing the road, hammering in a nail and ironing, for example.

☞ *Key points*

The major milestones in physical development are:

Gross motor development:

- head control
- sitting unaided
- crawling
- walking unaided.

Fine motor development:

- reaches out towards an object or person
- grasps an object with the whole hand (palmar grasp)
- manipulates small objects
- grasps an object between finger and thumb (pincer grasp)
- develops preference for right or left hand.

Cognitive development

By cognitive development, we generally mean:

- the ability to think and plan, that is to deal with things which are abstract
- the ability to learn
- the ability to deal with new situations.

Like physical development, cognitive development depends on the maturation of the brain, together with the opportunity to interact with the environment.

The child is born with a number of reflexes, most of which disappear as the brain develops, although a small number, such as 'jumping' at loud noises, continue throughout life. Early behaviours (actions) are simple, becoming more and more complex as the child gets older. As the brain develops and matures, she becomes more aware of her environment and more skilled in interacting with people and with the world around her. She acquires a vast amount of information. She stores what she has learned in her memory and builds up an astounding fund of knowledge, skills and abilities. She practises her new learning at every available opportunity, and continually refines her skills and adds to her knowledge. She is an explorer, a scientist and an adventurer, trying out her theories to see if they work, adapting them to suit different situations, finding out new things all the time and storing this knowledge for use in many different sorts of situations.

Milestones in cognitive development
The significant milestones in cognitive development are:

- awareness of cause and effect usually happens around the age of 3 or 4 months – for example, the baby learns that, if he moves his hand and hits a mobile hanging above him, he can make it move; if he cries loudly, he can make someone come to him
- imitation of other people's actions
- object permanence, that is awareness of the existence of objects and people even when they're absent, usually occurs around 7 or 8 months – for example, the baby can find a toy hidden under another one
- trial and error experimentation and problem-solving, that is trying out different ways of doing things to see what happens as a result, usually occurs at around 12 to 18 months
- thinking in symbolic (abstract) terms, that is the child can imagine that something is present, and can use something to represent something else – for example, a stick is used as a hairbrush, a leaf is used as a hat and the child laughs as he puts it on his head, aware that he is doing something funny. This stage is a particularly important one as it 'frees' the child from his immediate environment and is the beginning of the kind of thinking we rely on throughout life. This development usually starts in a simple way around 18 months and gradually becomes more refined as the child gets older.

☞ *Key points*

The major milestones in cognitive development are:

- **awareness of cause and effect**
- **imitation**
- **object permanence**
- **trial and error experimentation and problem-solving**
- **symbolic thought.**

Social and emotional development

As well as developing as a moving, thinking person, the child also learns to relate to those around her and become a sociable being. The part of the brain that will help her manage and control emotions is developing rapidly. Her interest in looking at faces is the beginning of socialisation. She learns that crying, smiling or making 'cooing' noises will get an emotional response from an adult, such as a smile and some conversation. She is becoming more accustomed to the world and is learning to handle the feelings which accompany everyday routines, such as anxiety, distress and excitement.

The child also starts to develop language, which will be one of the main tools of interaction with other people.

Milestones in social and emotional development

The major milestones in social and emotional development are:

- social responsiveness, which develops from about the age of 2 months – for example, the child will smile at human faces
- babbling, cooing, gurgling and laughing aloud, which usually starts at around 3 months
- awareness of herself as an individual, which begins at around 6 months
- the development of attachments to particular people, starting at about 7 or 8 months
- fear of strangers, from about 7 to 12 months
- recognition of simple words, her own name and names of people around her, at about 8 months
- first words, at around 8 to 10 months
- development of independence, from about 12 months
- understanding simple requests, at around 12 months
- naming of objects, at about 15 to 18 months
- putting words together – the beginning of sentences, starting around 18 months
- socialisation with others.

☞ *Key points*

The major milestones in social and emotional development are:

- social responsiveness
- awareness of self as an individual
- the development of language and the understanding of language
- the development of independence
- socialisation with others.

The effect of the environment

You may have noticed as you worked through the previous part of this section that the **child's interaction with the environment** is often referred to. The growth of the child's physical body and nervous system is extremely important, but the social and physical environment plays a huge part in his development.

What children see and hear around them, and the experiences they have, are crucial influences on their physical, cognitive, social and emotional development. So, an understanding of the part played by the child's environment, both social and physical, is vital for an understanding of growth and development.

The effect of the physical environment on growth and development

All children have certain basic needs that must be met if they are to grow and develop as they should. Some are obvious, such as the need for:

- healthy and nutritious food
- a satisfactory place to live
- protection from danger
- adequate clothing
- adequate hygiene
- protection from the weather.

In addition, children need opportunities to *interact* with the physical environment, and require:

- an interesting and stimulating environment
- physical activity and exercise
- space and opportunity in which to move around and explore the environment
- opportunities and equipment for play.

If these conditions are met, the child's growth and development is facilitated. If the environment does not provide these opportunities and experiences, the child's growth and development is hindered.

In children whose basic physical needs aren't met, physical growth may be restricted and they may be malnourished and prone to illness and disease. There are also other, less visible, effects. Adverse physical conditions affect the development of the central nervous system, hindering cognitive, social and emotional development.

The effects of the social environment on growth and development

In a similar way, the child's social environment can either facilitate or impede general development. The required conditions for optimum growth and development include:

- love, physical affection and attention
- a stimulating social environment which includes regular interaction with other people
- a sense of security
- a calm and ordered daily life, with predictable events
- strong relationships
- playmates and social stimulation
- a rich language environment, with verbal and social interaction.

Social environments which are impoverished will adversely affect a child's growth and development. Depending on the situation and the child's personality, adverse effects include:

- unruly, uncontrolled behaviours
- quiet and withdrawn behaviour
- withdrawal from social contact
- an inability to relate to people
- immature skill development for his age, such as not knowing how to play or under-developed language abilities
- an inability to understand spoken language
- immature motor skills, such as uncoordinated movements
- an inability to learn in the same way as other children of his age
- an inability to respond appropriately or make judgements, such as being unclear about what is required and unable to tell right from wrong and fact from fiction.

For most children, adverse environmental conditions can be rectified if the problems are identified early enough and steps are taken to remedy the situation. However, in extreme situations, where the emotional and social deprivation are acute and sustained, the effect on physical, social and emotional growth and development can affect the child for his entire life.

☞ *Key points*

The factors that facilitate individual growth and development in the physical environment are fulfilment of the child's basic needs.

The factors that facilitate individual growth and development in the social environment are:

• love and affection
• a stimulating environment
• security and predictability
• verbal and social interaction.

The factors that hinder individual growth and development in the physical environment are:

• neglect
• poor nutrition
• poor hygiene and sanitation
• exposure to danger.

The factors that hinder individual growth and development in the social environment are:

• neglect
• lack of love and affection
• a sterile social and emotional environment with limited opportunity for interaction with others.

Consider the effects of learning disability on each aspect of development

Like all other children, children with learning disabilities need love and support if they are to learn and develop to the best of their ability. And, just like all others, children with learning disabilities vary greatly from one another. Each is a unique human being with his or her own personality, talents, strengths and weaknesses. What they all have in common is a difficulty in their ability to learn and to deal with abstract thinking (cognitive development). Sometimes this is obvious at birth, but sometimes it is not.

People with a learning disability experience this difficulty in different ways, for different reasons and to different degrees. Sometimes physical development is also affected, sometimes not. Often, social and emotional development are affected, as a result of the cognitive difficulties. Compare the examples of Maria and Deepa below.

Examples

Maria and Deepa both attend a day centre for adults with learning disabilities.

Maria moves around by means of a wheelchair. She doesn't wheel it by herself, but is pushed by someone else. She communicates by making sounds, pointing at things or people and using her own gestures. She doesn't have much interest in doing stationary things, but enjoys music, cooking and eating. She shows her feelings by smiling and laughing when she is happy and by making loud complaining noises when she is upset. She has definite preferences for certain people and gets angry if they don't spend time with her.

Deepa is 'sporty' and in the athletic team at the day centre, which regularly takes part in competitions. She attends the centre three days a week and does voluntary work at an elderly person's home on the other two weekdays. She finds reading, writing and counting difficult and has not been able to master many of the skills she needs for everyday activities like travelling on the bus, doing her shopping or signing her name, so she tends to avoid situations which require these skills. She gets on particularly well with Gracie, her key worker at the centre, and with the manager of the residential home and likes to spend time with them, although this is not always possible. If she feels annoyed or neglected, she becomes very quiet and won't talk. It usually takes a long time to find out what is wrong with her.

In many ways, Maria and Deepa are very similar to one another and to any one of us. There are things they enjoy and things they dislike. They experience a range of emotions, getting happy, angry, upset, and so on. They also have their own ways of expressing emotion, which are similar to the rest of us: Maria makes a noise and Deepa goes into a 'mood'. They have their own strengths and weaknesses, like everyone else.

In common with one another, they have more **difficulties in learning** than most other people. These difficulties affect their ability to cope with everyday life. Maria's learning disability is obviously more severe than Deepa's.

In general, learning disability means that people:

- find it more difficult to learn things than most other people
- are slower to learn things and need more time to learn
- need more attempts at learning

- have greater difficulty remembering new things
- have greater difficulty in making use of their learning in new situations.

There are also many differences in the way in which learning disability affects different people. Here are some examples of the sorts of difficulties different people might have.

Some people have difficulty with **physical activity**, for example:

- some are unable to walk or to move around in any way by themselves
- some have problems with coordination, moving around in an uncoordinated way, bumping into things and often falling over
- some move much more slowly than is usual.

Speech and language can cause problems for some people, sometimes because of hearing loss, or sometimes for other reasons of growth and development of the central nervous system or a physical cause. For example:

- some people do not speak at all, or their speech might be difficult to understand
- some find it difficult to make sense of spoken language
- some speak in single words or in short phrases
- some speak rapidly and constantly, but to themselves and with little interaction with other people
- some have difficulty in making sense of noises, in finding out where noises come from or what they mean
- some people have very specific types of language problems which are complex and require the help of a speech and language therapist.

Activities which involve **visual skills or visual and motor skills combined** can be difficult for some people, for example:

- some people find it difficult to distinguish colour, shape or size
- some have problems knowing what it is they are expected to look at
- some people find it difficult to judge depth or distance.

Social and emotional skills pose problems for some people with learning disabilities, for example:

- some might have difficulties relating to people
- some might have problems understanding and/or expressing feelings
- some might have difficulties in controlling their moods or feelings and in responding in what is considered an 'adult' way
- some might form relationships too easily and trust people too readily

- some may show affection inappropriately, for instance, hugging someone they don't know well
- some may behave in ways that are considered 'anti-social' in the adult world, for instance, by showing challenging behaviours such as violent reactions.

One thing that may have crossed your mind as you read through all the examples above is that some of them don't just apply to people who have a learning disability. We all know people who express their feelings inappropriately, who sulk for days or who form relationships too quickly. Unfortunately, we are also too aware of the use of violence as a means of expressing feelings.

☞ *Key points*

Learning disability affects individuals in different ways:

- the severity of the learning disability varies from individual to individual
- some people have additional disabilities, such as a physical impairment or a sensory impairment, which can have an additional effect on their physical, social or emotional development.

Activity 2: The effects of learning disability on the individual

Think of someone with a learning disability whom you know well. Now list the kinds of difficulties this person has in relation to:

- *physical activities* ....

- *learning new skills*

- *remembering things*

- *social situations*

- *expressing or dealing with his or her feelings*

What does this tell you about how his or her learning disability has affected physical, cognitive, social and emotional development?

Comment

By being aware of the kinds of difficulties someone has in the different developmental areas, you will be able to tailor your support more effectively. You will probably be aware of the sorts of activities they find most challenging and, therefore, the developmental areas that are most affected by their learning disability:

- *activities involving motor skills (physical development), such as opening tins, manoeuvring a trolley around the supermarket, getting on and off buses quickly*
- *activities requiring social skills (social and emotional development), such as carrying on conversations, relating to a range of people*

- *activities requiring simpler or more complex thinking skills (cognitive development), such as remembering several things, planning for activities in the future, working out a solution to a problem.*

....

The effect of the immediate environment

Everyone will have cognitive difficulties of some sort, but some of these will be more severe than others. What you probably won't know is the extent to which their individual learning disability has been affected by their physical and social environment, and whether this has maximised their ability to learn or made their learning disability more severe.

Some of the difficulties people have *are* undoubtedly the result of their learning disability and have their roots in problems with the central nervous system. But the environment also plays a large part in how a learning disability affects each individual.

Children with learning disabilities need the same nurturing and stimulating environment as all other children in order to develop to the best of their ability. But they also need extra help with their physical, cognitive, social and emotional development from an early age. The more help and support they are given from the beginning, the more they will progress. Foundations laid down in early childhood pay dividends in later life for children with learning disabilities, just as they do for other children.

The effect of the wider environment

The importance of the *immediate* social and physical environment on the individual was discussed earlier – the family environment, for example. However, we must also take account of the *wider* social environment and its effect on the individual.

People with learning disabilities face prejudice and discrimination within society. This affects:

- their image of themselves, for example when they are seen as having less value than other people
- their confidence and self-determination, for example when they are perceived by others as incapable and dependent
- the opportunities that are made available to them – these are much more restricted than those of other people
- the extent to which they are included in mainstream activities and interact with their peers – they experience segregation and exclusion.

All of these have a profound effect on every aspect of their growth and development.

These issues are discussed more fully in the final section of this workbook and in the BILD workbook for *Positive Approaches to Anti-Oppressive Practice*.

How a knowledge of human growth and development relates to your work

You may be thinking to yourself at this stage, 'That's all very well, but how does this relate to me and my work?'. The answer is that the more you understand about the kinds of learning disability experienced by the people you work with, the better able you will be to help them deal with and overcome some of their difficulties. And one of the interesting things about new knowledge is that it has a 'multiplier' effect. In other words, the more you learn, the more you open up your own capacity for new learning. It works like this:

You become more skilled in understanding learning disabilities

You know what to look for

You begin to notice more, and so become more skilled in observation

You ask more questions and find more answers

**You build up more knowledge, which leads you on
to ask more questions ... and so it goes on**

All learning leads to other openings and possibilities.

Below are some suggestions for how a knowledge of human growth and development can help you find ways of supporting people's learning.

Become as skilled an observer as possible

Use your knowledge of the different aspects of physical, cognitive, social and emotional development to help you observe the kinds of difficulties people seem to have in these areas. A more informed knowledge will help you find the most appropriate ways of supporting learning.

Encourage people to discuss the difficulties they are having, whenever this seems appropriate

This takes a lot of sensitivity and should be done only when you have a good relationship with the person. Some people mistakenly believe that it's not right to discuss such difficulties, but many people with learning disabilities welcome the opportunity to talk about their learning problems providing this is done within a relationship of trust and respect. This enables you to work together to find ways of overcoming the difficulties.

Break learning down into small steps, and don't expect people to learn too much at one time

Analysing tasks into manageable steps, with one leading to another, is a common way of helping people with learning disabilities to learn things. But sometimes, even when we think we have made the steps small enough, people still have difficulty, so the steps might have to be even smaller.

Ask yourself if the person really needs to learn this

Sometimes things are done through habit. If there's no real need for someone to learn something, forget it.

Make learning as stimulating, meaningful and enjoyable as possible

Boredom makes for poor learning, for you and for the person you're working with. Be creative in the way you plan things.

When people have problems learning something, try approaching the task in a different way

Don't stick to the same old routine. Learning happens best when there's novelty and the right degree of challenge. The same supermarket every week can get boring. Try a new one.

Use what people know to help them learn more

New learning is built upon previous learning. People often feel safe with what they know and can do, so use this when it seems appropriate to help them move on. This sounds like a contradiction of the previous point, but use your own experience and judgement to decide when each one applies.

Seek specialist help when you see the need

It's easy to get used to a situation, especially when you've been working in the same place with the same people for some time. Try to look at things through 'new eyes' and decide whether someone else could help with the difficulty, such as a colleague, a speech and language therapist, a social worker or a psychologist for example. Work with this person, and the person with the learning disability, to find new solutions.

Section 2:
Changes in understanding about learning disabilities

Changes in understanding about learning disabilities

Introduction

The next part of the workbook deals with the changes which have occurred in our understanding of learning disabilities, and the impact this has had on services and the opportunities available to people.

The section deals with:

- the change from the philosophy of eugenics to that of empowerment
- the change from over protection to that of risk taking
- changes in attitudes towards relationships and sexuality
- the change from the philosophy of sterilisation to that of parenthood
- changes in expectations towards people with learning disabilities in relation to employment and housing.

From eugenics to empowerment

It's only fairly recently we've begun to talk about **empowerment** in relation to people with learning disabilities. To find out what it means and how it might happen, it's helpful to take a look at some of the reasons we've arrived at this stage.

Discrimination and oppression

The history of disabled people is one of discrimination and oppression. One of the most oppressive and inhumane movements was that of eugenics. Eugenics is based on the idea of the superiority of one group of people and the inferiority of another.

☞ *Key points*

Eugenics means trying to control the characteristics of a race by selective breeding. It is a philosophy based on the superiority of one race, or one dominant group of people, over another.

Even before the emergence of eugenics, people with learning disabilities were already being segregated in large institutions. This was a form of social control. The eugenics movement reinforced the stereotype of people with learning disabilities as a threat and further sanctioned their isolation and exclusion from mainstream society.

Photograph of two boys from the Shuttleworth Collection (Wellcome Institute Library)

As a result of this way of thinking, people with learning disabilities were:

- seen as 'undesirables' within society
- removed from families and communities and placed in large institutions
- (parents were often encouraged by doctors to 'put him away and forget you ever had him')

- segregated and isolated from other people
- denied their individuality and seen as all alike on account of their learning disability
- denied their freedom and any control over their own lives
- seen as asexual beings, without feelings.

The institutions were the province of the medical profession, since learning disability was seen as a medical 'problem'. All facilities were provided within the institution and there was no need for any of the 'patients' ever to go outside the doors.

Many of these institutions were located in isolated areas, to minimise the 'danger' to others. It was common for young children to be taken hundreds of miles away from their home area to live in one of these large hospitals. The traumatic effects of this practice were immense.

Example

Bill is 76 years old and remembers being taken to the long-stay hospital when he was about 4 or 5. *'Something happened to my mother, I think'* he told me, *'and they were afraid I might have trouble, so they put me in a bus and took me there.'* 'There' was a large institution almost 200 miles away from his home. He never saw any of his family again and doesn't know what happened to them, although there were unsuccessful efforts to trace relatives when he got out of the institution at the age of 72.

He remembers the long, long journey, *'feeling scared because of all the people there'* and having to *'sleep in a ward with loads of other children'*. *'They were very strict so you had to do what you were told, otherwise you got into big trouble.'*

'I'll never go back there, never, no matter what they do to me. I don't know why they took me away – I would have been alright – I could've looked after myself – got married and all that.'

Not all people with learning disabilities went into long-stay institutions, of course. Many stayed with their families. But large numbers lived in large institutions from birth until death, or until 'resettlement' programmes started in the late 1970s and people began to move back into the community.

Making changes

The impetus for change came from several sources:

- scandals about the dehumanising treatment of people within institutions
- a growing awareness of the rights of people with learning disabilities to have valued lives alongside the rest of the population

- the development of the 'ordinary life' movement, with its emphasis on ordinary houses and ordinary jobs for people with learning disabilities.

The same period saw the beginnings of the self-advocacy movement, initially in the US, and later in the UK. For the first time, there was acknowledgement of the fact that people with learning disabilities had:

- something to say
- the right to speak out and be listened to
- the right to make their own choices and decisions
- their own opinions and aspirations
- their own ideas about their own futures.

Which brings us, after a very brief summary of very complex developments over a considerable number of years, to the issue of empowerment.

Empowerment refers to the need for the **redistribution of unequally shared power** within our society. It is based on the recognition that:

- people with learning disabilities are disadvantaged within society
- that this disadvantage is largely the result of the way in which systems within society are designed and operate
- that this results in a denial of their basic human rights and excludes them from mainstream society
- that disadvantage must be eliminated
- that the empowerment of people with a learning disability, both individually and collectively, will facilitate the move towards their equality.

We can summarise the move from a philosophy of eugenics to a philosophy of empowerment like this:

Eugenics	⇒	**Empowerment**
People with learning disabilities considered as 'undesirable'	⇒	People with learning disabilities recognised as valued human beings
Segregation in institutions	⇒	Move towards inclusion in all walks of life
Individuality denied: collective 'solution'	⇒	Individual differences recognised: individualised responses
Controlled	⇒	Support to claim rights

This is not to say that people with learning disabilities have yet achieved empowerment and equality – far from it. But we have made *some* progress towards empowerment and away from eugenics.

For the individual, empowerment happens in a wide variety of ways:

- through access to information about things that concern you
- through belief in yourself
- through access to the same opportunities for education, housing, employment and leisure pursuits as other people in your community
- through achievement
- through making a contribution to society.

Empowerment for the *individual* person with learning disabilities is extremely important, but there is a wider issue – the need to deal with those aspects of our society that disempower *all* people with learning disabilities, which is based solely on the fact that they have learning disabilities.

☞ *Key points*

Empowerment is the redistribution of the balance of power which enables people with learning disabilities to take control of their own lives and achieve their full human and citizenship rights.

Activity 3: From eugenics to empowerment

Read back over Bill's story in the example above. Describe the ways in which our ideas have changed over his lifetime, away from the philosophy of eugenics towards a philosophy of empowerment. Describe this in terms of:

1. Bill's very early life when he was sent/taken away from home.
2. The moves we're now making to help people with learning disabilities become empowered.

Read through the information immediately above to help you with this activity.

....

....

....

....

....

....

Comment

Did you mention any of the following points?

1. Bill's early life:
- *people with learning disabilities considered 'undesirable' within society*
- *children removed from their families and communities*
- *children with learning disabilities placed in large institutions far from everyone else*
- *segregated from all other children for education*
- *lived collectively without any regard for their feelings or the effect on them*
- *no understanding of their individuality – they were all seen as alike because of their learning disability.*

2. What happens now:
- *acknowledgement of humanity and individuality*
- *recognition of the need to help people fight for their rights*
- *a move away from segregated services*
- *a move towards inclusion*
- *the self-advocacy movement*
- *moves towards greater control for people over their own lives.*

....

We still have a very long way to go until people with learning disabilities are truly empowered, although we have taken some steps towards empowerment. If you work in a service, you will probably be involved in self-advocacy in or service users' committees. If you are the parent or carer of someone with learning disabilities, you may be advocating on behalf of a son or daughter unable to speak up for him or herself, or you may be supporting your son or daughter in self-advocacy. As a parent or carer, you may also be contributing your own views to developments and new initiatives.

Comments on empowerment from the A&S Group

'Well, I feel that I've done something that I believe in, and now that I can stand up against the community, for disabled people, and also can tell some people what I think about them, in that way I'll stop them bullying disabled people and that.'

'Empowerment is a good thing and a bad thing. About two years ago, disabilities, disabled rights, that's a good empowerment. A bad one is, before that legislation came in, people with a learning disability got treated like rubbish, and had to fight barriers, but now since the whole action got taken along they make more noises than before.'

'Going out and being independent. Because a long time ago I wasn't independent – I was in the house all the time. I'd go to the club on a Friday, and the swimming every Thursday and Friday. That was when I was at my mum's – when I was at my mum and dad's. But now I've moved into Key Housing and I've got the flat. I'm independent now and that sort of thing.'

'The first time I came here – I'll tell you a wee story about a certain person … This girl, this lady called – said "I'm sorry, Andrew, I'm sorry, Andrew." This lady kept saying that all the time, until I told her one day, I said "Stop being sorry". I said "I don't want to hear it.". And since then – I've really passed this person a lot of confidence, and every time she has a problem or that, I say "I'll always be your shoulder".'

'My life is achievement – swimming, horse riding. If I see a person with a disability having a good time I feel great because I know that person with a disability is doing great.'

'Since we set this group up, it started seven years ago – because seven years ago I really didn't have any power at all. So that's why we decided to set this group up and this group has built from one small piece of a cake to a big, huge bit – and also a bit more – more freedom, and I'm not shut in a cage all day because I've got something to offer that no-one else can – that's to build up a future for Stirling and make Stirling a more, stronger voice – because I've got a lot of friends that I've kent [known] for years, and a lot of my friends that I've kent for years are in other parts of the country too and they're all in things themselves. They've actually learned from my bit, so I've got a very strong feeling about the whole nation – and it doesn't come from up there [indicates head] – it comes from like, the gut, in there. And if you've got that in there, you can share it, and that's the way I feel that I'm confident. I've got that in there, and it gives me confidence.'

'Power. A stronger voice – so that I can help you to cope when things go bad. And that's what makes me confident in myself, because I know that I can do it. I've achieved it. I've actually achieved a goal.'

For people with learning disabilities to be fully empowered, there will have to be radical changes in the fabric of society. Some of these changes will happen as a result of movements like self-advocacy. Others will require more legislation and more commitment, both social and political, than we have at present. But there are many things we can all do. No one person can empower another, but we can support people with learning disabilities in their struggle for empowerment.

From over-protection to risk taking

For most of us, risk taking is perceived as an integral part of everyday life, and an important one. As children move from infancy to early childhood, then school age, then adolescence, they are allowed by parents, and society as a whole, to take increasingly greater risks. It would be nonsensical to allow a two year old to wander in a busy street, but perfectly alright for a fourteen year old. However, most parents would be unhappy about a fourteen year old wandering the same street at two o'clock in the morning. We gradually assume more and more responsibility for our own actions as we grow from childhood into adulthood. The older we are, the less need there is for other people to protect us in ordinary everyday activities.

In this respect, as in many others in life, people with learning disabilities have traditionally been perceived as *different* by the rest of us in society, and, as a consequence treated differently. The prevailing attitude has been that:

- they are incapable of looking after themselves and must therefore be protected from risk by other adults;
- they are incapable of understanding risk or of dealing with it, so they must not be exposed to any risk if it can possibly be avoided.

This way of thinking has resulted in many people being *over protected* – not allowed to take part in the range of activities, or of social interactions, that adults would ordinarily have access to. Their experiences have been child, rather than adult, orientated, and often boring and undemanding. Because they have not had enough experience of risk, they have not learned to assess potential sources of risk or to develop strategies for deal with them. Some people have developed an unnecessary fear of anything which involves risk, often picked up from relatives, carers or staff.

Fortunately, much of this has started to change. As people with learning disabilities are increasingly being recognised as adults with adult rights and responsibilities, so our attitudes towards risk taking is slowly beginning to change. *Risk taking* is being recognised as an important part of learning in life. There is growing recognition that rights don't stop at a certain point, just because there is risk involved. Identifying, assessing and dealing with potential or actual risk is being built into more people's support plans.

☞ *Key points*

Traditionally, people with learning disabilities have been protected from risk, because of a mistaken notion that they are unable to understand potential risks, or to deal effectively with them. This resulted in the denial of equality of opportunity and of their rights as adults to control their own lives. More recently, there has been growing recognition of their adult status and their right to:

- experience risk
- develop appropriate strategies for dealing with risk
- learn from risk in the same way as other adults do
- be responsible for deciding on the level of risk they wish to experience in their own lives.

Changes in attitudes towards relationships and sexuality

People with learning disabilities have also had to contend with contradictory views of their sexuality. It was believed, on the one hand, that they were promiscuous and highly fertile, and on the other, that they were asexual, with no sexual feelings, needs or desires.

The same contradictory view existed towards sexual relationships. For example, there is evidence that sexual abuse was tolerated in some long stay institutions as long as it wasn't too obvious. This included both abuse of residents by staff and of residents by other residents. In some institutions, women were put on the contraceptive pill as a matter of course, without their consent, with the expectation that they were likely to engage in sexual relationships, willingly or unwillingly. At the same time, no attempt was made to provide sex education.

In some quarters it was also believed that people with learning disabilities didn't have the same feelings as everyone else, and so couldn't form attachments. They were considered as emotionally sterile, with sex considered merely as animal instinct.

Issues concerning sexuality and the sexual rights of people with learning disabilities are only just beginning to be recognised as part of the human rights agenda. The discussion is by no means straightforward and is overladen with ethical and moral contentions, such as attitudes towards contraception and abortion, sexual orientation and sex outside marriage.

Nevertheless, there has been some progress. For instance:

- the sexuality of people with learning disabilities is recognised, although prejudicial attitudes still exist in places;
- sex education is more likely to be made available to young people and adults and is considered an important part of education;
- there is a growing number of organisations dedicated to sexual issues for people with learning disabilities;
- specialist learning disability organisations such as Mencap and Enable are campaigning on issues relating to sexuality and sexual abuse;
- the sexual abuse of people with learning disabilities is being taken more seriously;
- there is much more support for people with learning disabilities who want to develop sexual relationships and/or live together;
- there is a much wider field of literature on sexuality and learning disabilities;
- there are many more specially designed teaching and learning materials dealing with sexuality and relationships.

☞ *Key points*

People with learning disabilities encountered discrimination and prejudice in relation to their relationship and sexual rights over a long period of time. Contradictory views of their sexuality held that they were, on the one hand, promiscuous and highly fertile, and on the other, that they were asexual, with no sexual feelings, needs or desires. They experienced the following oppression:

- Sexual abuse was often overlooked
- They were prevented from forming satisfactory sexual relationships and from getting married or living together.

Sex education was denied them and it was believed that they did not experience the same emotions as other people.

Currently, there is some progress. For example:

- Sex education is more widely available
- There is more recognition of their emotional and sexual rights and more support for the development of sexual partnerships and marriage
- Information relating to sexuality is more accessible to people with learning disabilities, their relatives or carers and practitioners.

From sterilisation to parenthood

Linked with changes in attitude towards relationships and sexuality is that of the right to parenthood, a right denied to people with learning disabilities for a very long time. One reason for this was the influence of the eugenics movement, discussed previously in this section, which took the view that people with learning disabilities would endanger the 'purity' of the race if they were 'allowed' to have children. But there were other reasons.

It was believed that parenthood would be an unsuitable role for people with learning disabilities because:

- they would probably have children with learning disabilities and this was undesirable
- this would put a greater strain upon the state
- they would not understand the responsibilities of parenthood
- they would be unable to look after a child and provide it with the love, care and stimulation it required.

Because of this, strict measures were taken to control the reproductive capacity of people with learning disabilities:

- men and women were segregated within the institutions and punished if they were found together
- drugs were used to control 'sexual urges' in men
- women were sterilised without their permission, and were put on the contraceptive pill when it became available, without their knowledge or consent

- women who did get pregnant had their pregnancies terminated
- those who had children often had their children taken away from them as a matter of course, regardless of their ability to cope.

However, there is a growing acceptance of the fact that people with learning disabilities have as much right to parenthood as anyone else.

People with learning disabilities should be supported in the role of parenthood because:

- they have a right to have children if they want to, as we all do
- there is plenty of evidence to show that many of those who have children make extremely good parents, if given appropriate support
- children should remain with their families unless this is totally impossible.

☞ *Key points*

Parenthood has been viewed historically as an unsuitable role for people with learning disabilities because:

- they were considered incapable of understanding the role of parenthood and of providing adequately for children
- it was believed that they would have disabled children, which was considered undesirable and a drain on state resources.

The reproductive capacity of people with learning disabilities was controlled by:

- segregation of the sexes within institutions
- sterilisation
- drugs
- enforced contraception
- abortion
- removing the child from them.

People with learning disabilities should be supported in the role of parenthood because:

- they have a fundamental right to parenthood, if they wish to have children, just as everyone else has
- given the appropriate support, they're capable of raising their children.

Comments on parenthood from the A&S Group

'Well, I would say that everybody, right, has a free choice, because this is a free country, right. We have the right to get married, have a family, have our own house, do what you want to do. No one's going to say to you "Oh, you can't do that, and you can't do this", but sometimes the workers interfere with it. They make matters worse. If you've got a relationship going, right, and you feel fine, if you say to your fiancée, right, let's start and have a family, right? Okay? And your fiancée gets pregnant. What happens? The worker finds out; they come down like a ton of bricks on you. They get the family involved, the police involved, and that's it. You're back to square one. So I think that if you start a relationship with a girl, workers should back off and leave it. Let you carry on the way you want to be.'

'I was going to say that if the supporting mechanism's there, if the couple want it, because even able-bodied couples have marriage break-ups and they end up homeless, so what is it going to be like if someone with a learning disability is homeless – it's not very nice, it's bad enough for an able-bodied person, right, if a marriage breaks up. So I think be cautious, take precautions, have a support mechanism. Some people don't have a family nearby, they live elsewhere, so they might not have family, they might not have friends, so who are they going to contact if there's going to be problems in the relationship? Well, one, if they are really, really 100% confident it would work, and two, if they find out before you commit to anything, you find out about any supporting mechanisms from anywhere that might come in a few hours a week to visit and see how well you're getting on until the couple feels comfortable that they can manage okay and they can leave a message if they need help.'

'I have a friend who lives in [names place and support service], who has a wee boy, he's 3. But because she's got a hand like that [demonstrates] – people thought she wouldn't be able to cope, that she wouldn't be able to look after the baby, that she wouldn't be able to do anything for that baby. But she said "I'll show them that I can". People should be able to show people what it's like to have a child when they want.'

'I'd love to get married and have children, but my mum and dad won't let me – I wish I had a child as well; but I can't have children at all. I was a wee bit disappointed – I would love to have a child. One of the women who comes to one of the committees has a wee baby, and when I see her I think, I wish that was me. I would love to have children. When I found out I couldn't have children I was – well, a wee bit disappointed.'

'Because we have learning disabilities it doesn't matter if we have a learning disabled child or not, as long as you're healthy , you don't smoke, you eat well, *eat healthily, and you do all this to protect your health, it doesn't matter if you have a disability or not a disability.*

'If you have a good sex life with your partner, right, and she gets pregnant, right, and it takes 9 months for the baby to be born, right – how can a doctor tell that the baby is going to come out disabled? No, it doesn't matter if the baby is born disabled. You're the one that brought it into the world; you should be proud, right? Right?'

Expectations in relation to housing and employment

Many of us would like to win the lottery, the football pools or the premium bonds and be able to live where we like and never have to work again. However, the reality for the vast majority is that we don't have this sort of choice. For people with learning disabilities, the choices are even more limited. The next activity leads us into a consideration of housing and employment for people with learning disabilities.

Housing

Activity 4: The importance of your own home

How important is it to you to have a home of your own, whether it's rented or bought? List all the things that are particularly important to you about your home.

....

....

....

....

....

....

Comment
You probably said at least some of the following:

- *a place of shelter and security*
- *somewhere I can relax*
- *somewhere I can indulge myself*
- *a place to spend time with family and friends*
- *somewhere I can be myself and not have to worry about the outside world*
- *somewhere I can make into the kind of place I like to live in*
- *a secure base from which I can do many things, including work.*

And many other things.
....

Five of the members of the A&S Group who contributed to this workbook live in their own homes. Three live in houses owned by a specialist housing association and two live in council houses with their own tenancy. One woman shares a flat; the other five people live on their own, through choice.

Idem would like to move, not because he doesn't like his flat, but because he has few friends of his own age where he lives. Plans are underway but it will take some time, he tells me. David is very happy with his council house and enjoys his garden. He loves animals, has three pets and helps out at an animal shelter on a regular basis.

The people in the A&S Group still have more limited choices than some of us, but more than many other people with learning disabilities. And certainly far more than they would have done 20 or 30 years ago.

Limited choice
Before the 'resettlement' programme mentioned earlier, the choice for the vast majority of people with learning disabilities would have been:

- a long-stay hospital
- a hostel
- at home with relatives.

There was little recognition of the fact that they might have the same aspirations as other people and want to have their own home, either alone or with someone of their own choosing – a partner or a friend, for instance. The hospital closure and resettlement programmes opened up new opportunities although, in many places, thinking was still limited. For example, people were 'trained' in the hospitals in order to prepare them for life outside and in some places were not allowed to move out until they had been assessed as 'ready'. As one university student remarked, thinking of the state of her college residence, 'I'd fail every one of the tests and never be allowed out!'.

Although hospital closure was a huge step forward, there was a dawning realisation that merely placing people in the community in ordinary houses did not guarantee them their full rights as ordinary citizens and equal people. In addition, many of the institutionalised practices which were prevalent in the hospitals were, in some cases, merely imported into smaller community-based establishments. In effect, people still had very limited choice and limited control over their own lives. In general, they had to go where they were put.

The emergence of new forms of residential accommodation

In the early period of resettlement, several forms of housing options emerged:

- 'core and cluster', where a central house provided support to smaller units within close proximity
- staffed hostels for people judged able to do a certain amount for themselves
- residential homes for people who were considered to need full-time support
- staffed group homes for between two and six people
- respite care facilities where people living with families could spend a short period of time
- full-time or part-time support for people living in their own homes, either alone or with a friend or partner.

While some of these options were an improvement on the large institutions, there were still many limitations including:

- importing the practices of the institutions into staffed houses and hostels; there was often reference to 'mini-institutions', run for workers instead of the people who lived there
- the choice of where to live was limited, so people really had very few options
- many people had to share houses with people they hadn't chosen to live with

- some houses had mixed sexes; when there were problems, especially of sexual abuse by a male resident, the woman was usually the one who was moved out
- there was limited opportunity to move on to another house
- people were 'residents', not tenants
- some group homes were redesignated as hostels, and rules applied which interfered with individual privacy and freedom; some of this was the result of legal requirements, but some was through workers importing hospital routines into what should have been ordinary housing.

Wider options

While many of these problems persist today, there is beginning to be a wider range of options and some organisations are doing innovative work. Much of what has happened owes its origins to the Ordinary Life movement of the 1980s, which first brought atrocities and inequalities to public notice and paved the way for other developments.

We've made some progress, especially in the following areas:

- more people are getting the choice of where to live and who to live with
- more people are living alone and getting the necessary support
- more people are getting tenancy agreements
- fewer people are being 'put through hoops', in order to prove that they can manage on their own.

But the following areas are still problematic:

- there are still people in long-stay hospitals
- there are still people having to live with others they wouldn't choose to live with
- there are people living alone or with others who do not receive the support they need
- there is still a great deal of controversy about residential communities and residential homes
- there are still a great many lonely people with learning disabilities
- people with learning disabilities still face prejudice and discrimination in their own homes.

☞ *Key points*

Historically, our expectations towards people with learning disabilities in relation to housing was that they would either live with their families all their lives or in long-stay institutions which were isolated and provided all amenities on the premises.

At the present time we recognise that people with learning disabilities:

- have the same aspirations as the rest of us for a home of their own
- have a right to their own home
- should have access to a range of housing options according to their needs
- have a right to choose where to live and who to live with
- are entitled to the type and level of support they require to live as independently as possible.

From *Scottish Executive (2000) The Same As You? A Review of Services for People with Learning Disabilities*
Home ownership is a good option for some people with learning disabilities. Ownership Options in Scotland:

- *helps people with disabilities overcome barriers*
- *provides a consultancy service*
- *provides financial help and advice*
- *arranges maintenance and is a link between those looking for property and potential buyers.*

From *Department of Health (2001) Valuing People: A New Strategy for Learning Disability for the 21st Century*
'People with learning disabilities can live successfully in different types of housing, from individual self-contained properties, housing networks, group homes, and shared accommodation schemes, through to village and other forms of intentional community. They can cope with the full range of tenures, including home ownership.' (p.70)

Employment

Activity 5: How important is your job to you?

Make a list of all the benefits you can think of which come from having a job.

Comment

Which of the following answers are similar to yours?

- *Money makes many other things possible.*
- *A job gives us status within society; it's no accident that people ask one another, often on early acquaintance, 'What do you do?', meaning what job of work do they do.*
- *Having a job makes us feel worth something.*
- *A job provides us with opportunities for companionship and for making friends, some of whom we spend time with outside of work.*
- *A job can lead on to other things, such as being on committees or representing our workmates in negotiations.*
- *Employment experience can help towards career advancement.*
- *A job can provide us with purpose and routine.*
- *Worthwhile employment can enable us to recognise and develop our own talents and abilities.*
- *Work can lead on to opportunities for further training and achievement.*

Now, let us think of how the aspects of employment in Activity 5 relate to people with a learning disability. Activity 6 will draw on your own knowledge and experience.

Activity 6: Employment and people with learning disabilities

Think of the people with learning disabilities you work with now or have worked with in the past.

Are any of them:	Yes	No
In full-time paid jobs in the open market?	☐	☐
In part-time paid jobs in the open market?	☐	☐
Doing voluntary work in place of a real job?	☐	☐
In a supported employment scheme?	☐	☐
In a job placement as part of job training?	☐	☐
Working in a sheltered workshop?	☐	☐
Working in the service and getting a wage?	☐	☐
Getting a good wage?	☐	☐
In a situation with possibilities for promotion?	☐	☐
Getting access to further training in their job?	☐	☐

Comment

There's a good chance that you'll have said 'yes' to at least some of these questions, unless you are working with people whose learning disabilities are extremely severe and complex. If the same questions had been asked 20 or 30 years ago, there would almost certainly have been far fewer ticks for 'yes'.

However, if we were to then to ask how many people have full-time jobs on the open market with good wages and opportunities for promotion and for moving on to other jobs, the answers would be very different.

The need for real jobs

When people with learning disabilities are asked about their aspirations, two things appear high on the list – a real job and a home of their own.

Some progress has been made, in relation to employment, just as in housing and other areas of life. Compared to the past we now have:

- a recognition that people with learning disabilities have a right to work, the same as everyone else
- more services actively involved in supporting people's search for work
- more specialist employment agencies
- more opportunities for work placements
- more opportunities for people to do voluntary work
- more mainstream employment organisations and services including people with learning disabilities.

Ultimately, we hope that as many people as possible, who want to work and who are fit for work, will be able to find work. In that respect, at least, our expectations towards people with learning disabilities have changed. Let's hope that the change continues, because opportunities for real work for most people with learning disabilities are still few and far between.

From *Scottish Executive (2000) The Same As You? A Review of Services for People with Learning Disabilities*
'Many people with learning disabilities want a decent job. They want to get on in life and have friends at work. The Scottish Executive's social inclusion strategy ranks having a job high in the list of measures to help people to be included in society. Employment has, so far, rarely been an option for people with learning disabilities. If they are to be usefully included in society, that has to change.'

From *Department of Health (2001) Valuing People: A New Strategy for Learning Disability for the 21st Century*
'The reasons for this exclusion from the labour market are complex, but they include:

- *Low expectations on the part of many agencies and professionals of what people with learning disabilities can achieve. This has meant that many learning disabled young people have not received training and preparation for employment. Services working with adults with learning disability have not seen helping them find work as a priority.*
- *The interaction between social security benefit rules and employment can result in disincentives to work for some learning disabled people.*
- *Difficulties in progressing from supported employment schemes (where they exist) into mainstream employment.' (p.84)*

Comments on employment from the A&S Group

'At the end of the day it's yourself. You try to get a full-time job. They don't want to know. Because you're labelled as disabled. We can't earn a decent wage. Some employers don't want to have you. Benefits are a problem. You can't earn more.'

☞ *Key points*

Historically, our expectations towards people with learning disabilities in relation to employment was:

- that they were incapable of 'real' jobs
- that occupational therapy or 'training' was more suitable for them.

At the present time we recognise that people with learning disabilities:

- have a right to a paid job of work
- should have a range of employment options
- are entitled to the support they require to find and keep a job of work.

Section 3:
The person, not the disability

The person, not the disability

Introduction

This section deals with the causes of learning disability and discusses:

- the importance of the individual, rather than the syndrome or condition
- the difference between congenital and environmental causes of learning disability
- heredity and learning disability
- multi-causation and learning disability
- the causes of learning disabilities and the effect on attitudes
- accessing literature and information for report-writing.

The person, not the syndrome

Knowing the cause of a particular learning disability can be useful, totally irrelevant or even harmful.

It can be useful to have certain information about cause when:

- this knowledge will enable you to provide better opportunities and support for the person
- a family member wants to know about a particular syndrome in order to understand what causes it and how they can best support a relative
- a person with a learning disability wants more information, or wants to join a support group; parents and professionals might also want contact with a support or information group. (Support and information groups are discussed in more detail later in this section.)

However, the cause of a learning disability is irrelevant much of the time because you are working or living with a *person*, not a condition or a syndrome.

Sometimes workers become too caught up in the idea of the syndrome, or cause, and lose sight of the person. Sometimes, even nowadays, people are referred to in terms of their syndrome, or condition, such as 'Are there any Downs?'. This denies the humanity and individuality of the person referred to. It also influences attitudes and perceptions.

Example

When Marius starts shouting and being generally abusive, his 'condition' is blamed. No-one has ever stopped to think that he might be angry because everything he does is controlled by other people or that he has never been helped to find more acceptable ways of expressing and dealing with his anger.

There are other dangers in concentrating on the syndrome, not the person.

- It can lead you to look for certain characteristics or behaviours and to believe you see them in people, even when they don't exist.
- It results in **labelling** of those with certain syndromes, for example talking about 'a Downs baby' or asking 'How many Downs are there?'
- It also results in **stereotyping**, for example the most common is the stereotype of people with Down syndrome – believing that they 'are always affectionate and like music'.
- It **compartmentalises** people, grouping them according to their syndrome, rather than seeing them as unique individuals in the same way as we see everyone else.
- It **dehumanises** the person.

The section which follows:

- gives you more background information about the main causes of learning disabilities, which should help you understand better the types of learning disabilities people might have
- will enable you to help those you work with to avoid any unnecessary risks
- will safeguard the people you work with and yourself in the work situation by ensuring that you are aware of any medical or practical difficulties associated with particular syndromes or conditions.

☞ *Key points*

It is essential that we always see the person, not the syndrome.

Concentrating on the syndrome and not the person means that we are:

- labelling the person concerned
- dehumanising them
- compartmentalising them according to their syndrome, rather than seeing them for the unique individuals they are.

Comments on labels from the A&S Group

'Labels are my downfall. I want to do a lot of things I can't do. Go to college. Be a nurse. I can't do it. Can't do anything I want to do. Not very good at it. Not good at writing and reading.'

'Labels are discrimination. Labelling somebody is discrimination. Robs you of your dignity.'

Congenital and environmental causes of learning disability

Learning disabilities can have either **congenital** or **environmental** causes.

Congenital causes

Congenital refers to learning disability that is present at birth, regardless of causation. The events that cause congenital learning disability happen *before birth*, when the foetus is developing in the womb. Events before birth include things like:

- an illness experienced by the mother while pregnant, such as rubella (German measles)
- genetic factors, such as Down syndrome
- personal habits, such as excess alcohol intake, smoking or substance abuse (drug-taking) and poor nutrition
- occupational hazards, such as exposure to radiation and certain chemicals
- poor living conditions, such as malnutrition or water pollution
- certain types of medication
- trauma or accident to the mother, such as a car crash, or a severe fall.

Environmental causes

Environmental causes of learning disability refer to causation *during* or *after birth*.

Events *during* birth that might cause learning disability, include:

- lack of oxygen to the child's brain can cause cerebral palsy which sometimes, but not always, causes learning disability
- problems when the foetus becomes distressed and sometimes when forceps are involved
- very premature births
- multiple births.

Causes which arise from events *after* birth include:

- social causes, such as severe neglect, which can affect the developing child's physical, cognitive and social development
- *trauma* ie, external incidents or accidents which affect the child's development, eg,
    - ⇨ road traffic accidents or accidents around the home
    - ⇨ severe illness eg, meningitis, or measles, which can cause intellectual impairment as well as hearing and visual impairment
    - ⇨ physical abuse.

It's important to keep this information in perspective. The percentage of children who have impairments as a result of incidences before, during or after birth is very small compared to the numbers born without impairments or who do not fully recover from accident or illness.

Hereditary and learning disability

Learning disability can also have *hereditary* causes. *Heredity* refers to the transmission of genes from one or both parents to the child. Down syndrome, Fragile X syndrome, Hurler's syndrome and Cri Du Chat Syndrome are examples of syndromes with hereditary causes.

With hereditary conditions, the condition or syndrome may or may not have occurred in the family previously. Some hereditary conditions affect only boys, others affect both sexes. Sometimes the woman is the carrier, sometimes the father. In some conditions, all children are likely to be affected. In others, the possibility is more random, and there is no certainty that a child will or will not be affected.

Where a condition or a syndrome is known to be or thought to be hereditary, the parents are likely to be offered genetic counselling.

Although great strides have been made in understanding the composition and function of genes, genetics is an extremely complex science and there is still a great deal we don't know about it. It is also very controversial.

☞ *Key points*

Learning disabilities can have congenital, environmental or hereditary causes.

***Congenital* refers to learning disability which is present at birth, regardless of causation.**

Hereditary refers to the transmission of genetic material from one or both parents.

Environmental refers to external incidents which occur during or after birth.

Incidents during birth include:

- lack of oxygen to the child's brain
- problems when the foetus becomes distressed and sometimes when forceps are involved
- very premature births
- multiple births.

Incidents after birth include:

- social causes, such as severe neglect
- trauma, which is the result of an external incident or accident, of severe illness or of abuse.

Multi-causation

Example

James was abandoned when he was a few months old. His mother had mental health problems. She tried her best, but was unable to cope, especially since she was on her own with James. One day she walked out of the flat in which they lived and just kept on going. By the time James was found he'd been on his own for several days and doctors were amazed that he was alive at all. He was severely malnourished and dehydrated, with signs that he'd been like this before being left alone. He had sores all over his body and cried only weakly. He showed signs of severe trauma.

By the time he was 5 and living with an adoptive family, James was doing reasonably well, but still had some difficulty. He was small for his age, his speech was very difficult to understand and he spoke in very short sentences. In school, he had trouble settling down to anything and had a very short concentration span. He desperately wanted to be friends with the other children and they quickly learned to put the blame on him if anything went wrong. He was very suggestible, so the other boys would 'dare' him to do things and he'd get caught in the act. So, he was always in trouble. He found school work very difficult and so was bored most of the time in class, which meant that he needed lots of attention from the teacher. Since there were 44 children in the class, this was difficult, and James more often than not got up to something which caused him more trouble.

Activity 7: Multiple causes

Read through James's story once more and then answer the questions below.

1. *What do you think was the cause of James's learning disability?*
2. *What is the reason for his over-eagerness to relate to the other children? Is it because:*
   * *he's always left out and wants to be included?*
   * *he is much more immature than other children and relates on a different level, needing their attention all the time?*
   * *his own self-image was damaged as a result of his early experiences?*

1 ____

____

____

____

2 ____

____

____

____

Comment
Question1
Did you suggest any of the following as contributory factors?

* *He could have had an impairment anyway, even before the trauma of separation from his mother, before or during his birth.*

- *It might have been drugs his mother may have been taking to help her deal with her illness.*
- *It could have been the trauma of separation from his mother, the primary caregiver.*
- *Perhaps it was malnourishment and dehydration.*

It's impossible to know, isn't it, although we can make informed guesses. Perhaps his mother was taking medication for her illness and this affected his development in her womb. Perhaps he had some sort of congenital disorder caused by something else, from his mother's genes, or his father's or a combination of both. Perhaps not. Perhaps it was the emotional trauma or the malnutrition and dehydration. More likely, it was a combination of at least some of these things.

Question 2
Without knowing James personally, it's difficult to say, isn't it? It could be any or all of the reasons listed. You may even have come up with an entirely different one. Whatever the reason, we know that James's previous experience has definitely had an effect on his present behaviour.

*Many learning disabilities have **multiple causes**. There might be a primary impairment, but the learning disability can be aggravated by other factors – congenital, hereditary and environmental factors.*

There are substantial limits on our understanding of the causation of any type of learning disability, and this is likely to be the case for a long time to come. In many situations there is simply no explanation of why and how an impairment might have occurred. Even with the syndromes and conditions we know something about, there are still many unknowns.

☞ *Key points*

Multi-causation refers to the situation when a learning disability is caused by a combination of congenital, hereditary and environmental factors.

Although our knowledge has increased, we are still limited in our understanding of many of the causes of learning disability because:

- we still have great deal to learn about genetics, which limits our understanding of hereditary factors in learning disabilities

- in the rapidly changing world in which we live, we are constantly being exposed to chemicals and pollutants, the effects of which we know nothing about
- multi-causation is extremely complex and therefore difficult to understand.

How the cause of a learning disability may affect society's attitudes

The way in which individual people, and society in general, perceive and respond to people with learning disabilities can be affected by the cause of the learning disability. For example, there are often different reactions towards someone with a learning disability in which:

- there is an obvious syndrome or condition, eg, Down syndrome
- the disability is the result of an illness
- there is no known cause.

As practitioners working with people with learning disabilities, or as parents or carers, we need to be aware of the myths, wrong information, attitudes and perceptions that often surround learning disability, in order that we can work to combat them.

The way in which society's attitudes differ according to the cause of the learning disability is discussed below in relation to the different causes.

Responses to a particular syndrome or condition

Society's reaction to people with particular syndromes or conditions generally involves:

- sadness and pity for the individual and his parents
- sympathy for the person, and usually her family, at the misfortune that has befallen them
- regarding them as less deserving than 'normal' people, because they are 'abnormal'.

Responses to a learning disability caused by illness

In contrast, there is usually a different reaction towards a learning disability that results from illness like meningitis, for example. A child who becomes disabled for this reason at the age of 5 will evoke a very different reaction from a child with a congenital disability. This reaction is sometimes referred to as the 'personal tragedy' of disability. The basis of this reaction is that the child was previously 'normal' and is somehow no longer 'whole' – less of a person than she was before. Society's attitudes are generally:

- sadness that this person is no longer 'whole'
- empathy for the person and the parents
- that the person is deserving of whatever help and support is available, because he was once 'normal', just like the rest of us.

Responses to a learning disability with no known cause

Where the cause of the disability is unknown and not obvious, there may be:

- hostility towards the parents from other family members
- guilt on the part of one or both parents
- blame as one parent blames the other, either silently or in words, or in-laws lay blame on the other side; there can sometimes be cultural complications, especially if the child is a boy
- in some religions, the belief that the parents are being punished for something in their past
- suspicions from other people about the cause of the disability, such as something hereditary or something the parents have done during the pregnancy.

It is clear that all the attitudes discussed above are not only ill-informed, but also discriminatory and damaging, to families and carers, and to the person with a learning disability. To return to the first point in this section, it is the *person* who is important. We don't ignore or deny the learning disability. The disability is an important part of the individual, just as her personality, height and other personal characteristics are also important. But we recognise the *individuality*, *uniqueness* and *value* of the person, just as we do with people who do not have learning disabilities.

Why society's attitudes differ in this way

These reactions arise from the fact that our society is based upon a mistaken notion of something which is thought of as *normality*. Everyone in society is judged against this idea of 'normality'. The further away you are from what is perceived as 'normal', the more you are seen as 'different' and less than perfect. Since normality, in this sense, means 'non-disabled', anyone who doesn't fit the picture is judged as inferior.

People who were never 'normal', eg, people with Down syndrome, are to be pitied, but since they were never 'normal' anyway, they are less deserving than people who *were* once 'normal', just like the rest of us. The 'tragedy' for parents is different, because they once had a 'normal' child.

☞ *Key points*

Attitudes towards people with learning disability may differ according to whether the cause is congenital, the result of accident or illness, or completely unknown.

Society's attitudes towards someone with a particular syndrome or condition usually involve:

* sadness
* sympathy
* a belief that this person is less deserving than other people because they are seen as 'abnormal'.

Society's attitudes towards someone whose learning disability is the result of illness are generally:

* sadness
* empathy for the person and the parents
* a belief that the person is deserving because he was once 'normal' and like the rest of us.

Society's attitudes towards someone whose learning disability has no known cause might involve:

* hostility towards the parents from other family members
* guilt or blame on the part of one or both parents or other family members
* in some religions, the belief that the parents are being punished for something in their past
* suspicions from other people about the cause of the disability, such as something hereditary or something the parents have done during the pregnancy.

Society's attitudes differ in this way because:

* people's attitudes are shaped by a mistaken and discriminatory perception of 'normality' which excludes large numbers of people, including all disabled people
* learning disability is viewed as a 'tragedy' for the person and her family, which is perceived differently according to whether

or not this person could once be characterised as 'normal' within this restricted concept of normality.

As practitioners working with people with learning disabilities, we need to be fully aware at all times that it is the person who is important regardless of the disability or its cause.

Accessing literature and information to write a report

We close this section by discussing situations in which you might have to produce a report about the causation of learning disability. For example, you might have to find out about a particular syndrome or condition for a specific purpose, such as providing more information to colleagues or developing your own understanding of learning disability.

The suggestions given here are starting points for your own research of the available literature and other information. Where you live will influence what is available to you to some extent. However, this is less of a problem than previously because of the internet which offers a wealth of information.

Libraries

Libraries are the most traditional sources of information. People vary in the extent to which they use libraries, so here are some tips for using them to best effect. If you are a regular and informed library user, you'll know these already.

- If libraries scare you, don't worry. Ask the librarian if you are having trouble finding something or are unsure of how the books are organised – that's what he or she is there for. Don't worry about being thought stupid – it's usually the most informed and most confident people who *do* ask questions.
- Be aware that, since libraries have to cover a wide range of topics, they are likely to have only a few books on the topic you're interested in – and maybe none at all.
- You can request books from other libraries although they may take some time to come.
- Avoid books that are very out of date as they may be incorrect and misleading. You should be able to tell from the tone of the writing and the way in which people with learning disabilities are described – use your own judgement. Always check the publication date of the book. You will find this somewhere within the first few pages, on the same page as the copyright details and often the publisher's name and address.
- Information about disability is likely to be distributed under several sections in the library collection – education, sociology, psychology and medical

sections, for instance. Don't forget the reference section in the library, but note that you won't be able to borrow books from here – you'll have to use them in the library.

- Avoid literature that describes people with learning disabilities as if they were medical 'specimens' instead of real people.
- If you cannot find what you want in your local library, some college and university libraries will allow you to join if you are studying a recognised course. You will probably have to pay a fee for this service; however, if you are doing your NVQ or SVQ through a local college, the college may have an arrangement with the university library or they may be prepared to arrange one.

The British Institute of Learning Disabilities (BILD), which publishes this workbook, has a library and an extensive range of information about learning disability that can be obtained from books, journals and reading lists. Details of how you can obtain this information are given at the back of this workbook. BILD also has a website at: www.bild.org.uk.

Specialist organisations

There are many specialist organisations that deal with learning disabilities in general or with specific syndromes or conditions. These range from large well-known charities such as Enable in Scotland and Mencap in England, Wales and Northern Ireland to small self-help groups run by parents and other volunteers.

Remember that groups like these get hundreds of requests, as you will know if you are involved in any way. Be reasonable with your request and be prepared to pay for postage and/or for the information, as costs mount up. Small organisations are poor and all organisations prefer to spend their money on people. The larger ones may have budgets for public information services, so may have factsheets and related information.

The internet

The internet has made much more information more readily available. If you do not have access to the internet at home, you should be able to use it at your local library, unless you are in a rural area served by a mobile library. In this case, perhaps you can get access at work, or through a neighbour. Internet cafés, which are becoming more common all the time, also provide you with possibilities.

If you have not yet used the internet, it isn't as mysterious as it sounds. Once you have learned a few basic procedures, it's easy and it opens up many possibilities, especially if you're studying, so be prepared to give it a go. Remember that the more precise you can be about what you are searching for, the easier, less time-consuming and less costly the task.

The following websites are useful starting points:

Foundation for People with Learning Disabilities

www.learningdisabilities.org.uk

Paradigm	www.paradigm-uk.org
Mencap	www.mencap.org.uk
BILD	www.bild.org.uk
Down's Syndrome Association	www.dsa-uk.com
Department of Health	www.doh.gov.uk
Scottish Executive	www.scotland.gov.uk
National Assembly for Wales	www.wales.gov.uk

Writing a report on the causation of a learning disability in relation to a service user

Before you get started on your report, you need to do some planning so that you will make the best possible use of your time. Good planning is crucial. If you know what you're looking for and why, you won't waste time and you'll avoid getting lots of irrelevant information.

Step 1: Planning

1. Be absolutely clear about the purpose of your report, for example to submit for a course, to circulate to other workers, to use for a talk.

2. Write down your objectives, for example:

   (i)   To find out about the cause of Asperger's syndrome.

   (ii) To describe the relevance of this information for those working with people with Asperger's syndrome.

3. Plan the structure of your report, for example:

   (i)   A brief introduction stating what the report is about and what the purpose is.

   (ii) A brief description of the syndrome or condition.

   (iii) Details of the cause of the syndrome or condition (this will be the main part of the report).

   (iv) Any other relevant information. (Don't include details just because you have discovered them, unless they have a purpose in the report.)

   (v)   A paragraph or two about the relevance and/or implications of the cause for people living and/or working with the person, for instance why it is important for practitioners to have this information and how it can help in their work etc. (This section will be influenced by the reason why you are writing the report.)

(vi) Concluding comments: a closing paragraph rounding off the report and making a statement which brings it to a close.

(vii) Details of the sources of your information, for instance leaflets from organisations, libraries, etc, book references, website addresses.

(viii) Names and addresses of organisations, if appropriate.

Planning is *never* time wasted, so plan well. Badly planned or unplanned written work will never do justice to your efforts, no matter how hard you work in finding things out.

Step 2: Researching the information

Plan how you will go about this:

- Where are your best sources? Use these first.
- Do you have to send off for information? Get this done in plenty of time.
- How long will it take and how much time do you have realistically?
- If you have access to the internet, make an early start with this as it may save you going elsewhere. Assess the reliability of the websites you are using; cross-check with other websites. Don't spend time going through lots of irrelevant detail or downloading information you don't understand – for instance, medical sites are likely to be full of medical jargon which is incomprehensible to most of us; it's much better to use a site from a recognised organisation such as Mencap, Enable, BILD, Capability Scotland or Scope and one in which parents are involved or have started themselves.
- If you are using books, photocopying relevant passages and using a highlighter pen will save you making reams of notes.

Step 3: Writing the report

- Pace yourself. Don't try to do it all at once; give yourself breathing space.
- Once you have written the first draft of the report, leave it for a few days and then go back to it. Go through it making the necessary changes and write your second draft. Repeat as necessary with subsequent drafts.
- It's a good idea to read things aloud to yourself as this helps you hear mistakes and parts that don't flow so smoothly.
- Always try to type your report, or get someone else to type it for you; most places require this nowadays.

Section 4:
Expectations, information and experiences

Expectations, information and experiences

Introduction

This section deals with:

- the danger of inappropriately limiting expectations of individuals with particular syndromes or conditions
- understanding when and why it might be important to be able to identify the possible effects of some syndromes or conditions
- researching information about the possible effects of particular syndromes or conditions
- understanding the role of support groups.

The danger of expectations

Use the following activity to help you think about the part that expectations play in everyday life.

Activity 8: Expectations

What are your expectations in the following situations?

1. Going into the supermarket where you usually do your shopping.

....

....

....

2. Phoning a friend to suggest meeting in the pub for a drink that evening.

....

....

....

3. Getting home from holiday and finding the house in a complete mess, with everything all over the place.

....

....

....

4. Your line manager says 'Can you come to my office? There's something I need to discuss with you.'

....

....

....

5. A police car turns up at your door one evening.

....

....

....

Comment
You might have said something like the following to each situation.

Question 1: I'd expect:
- *everything to be in the same place as before*
- *to be able to do my shopping as always*
- *that they might have moved things round and it would take me longer than usual*
- *to be able to buy what I wanted*
- *it would cost me a lot.*

Question 2: I'd expect:
- *s/he would or would not be able to come*
- *s/he'd suggest an alternative*
- *no answer or someone else to answer.*

Question 3: I'd expect:
- *that I'd been burgled*
- *my son or daughter had been having a party – there'd be trouble*
- *I wouldn't know what to expect.*

Question 4: I'd expect:

- *trouble!*
- *something had happened to someone and it's serious*
- *s/he wants me to do something and I'm not going to like it.*

Question 5: I'd expect:

- *something's happened and they're coming to my door!*
- *it must be for someone else*
- *my husband/wife/partner was popping home for something, if s/he is in the police*
- *one of my children is in trouble.*

Your expectations would depend on your own situation and lifestyle, and on the circumstances.

Expectations are an ordinary part of our lives. We are constantly predicting what will happen. This helps us to deal with life and to plan (for example the family will be home for dinner tonight, so I'll make lasagne). Our world is largely predictable and our ability to know what to expect saves us from constant anxiety. One of the reasons why exotic holidays and adventure holidays are so popular is that we *don't* know what to expect, so there is a sense of excitement and exhilaration. So expectations are generally very positive things.

However, expectations can also have *negative* effects, as shown by the example below.

Example

Stan met a new parishioner at church and welcomed him warmly. The man was Asian, probably from Pakistan, thought Stan. 'Are you working on the buses?' he asked. 'No' replied the man, 'I'm a surgeon at the infirmary'.

There was no malice in Stan's questions, but his expectations were shaped by a racial stereotype. There had been many immigrants into the city over recent years and many worked as bus drivers or conductors – some because they were waiting to have their qualifications approved.

Expectations of people with learning disabilities have a strong influence on how we relate to them and what we expect of them. Look at the next example.

Example

Alison, a new young teacher in special education, was told in the 1970s: 'Mentally handicapped children can't learn to read, so there's no point in trying to teach them'. So she didn't, and guess what? None of the children learned to read!

One of the real dangers of knowing about a particular syndrome or condition is that it can limit your expectation of people. This can have several consequences.

- If you think the person won't be able to respond, it can prevent you making certain opportunities available to them.
- It can lead you to look for *inabilities* rather than abilities.
- It can cause you to see problems that don't exist.
- It can make you expect certain types of behaviours.
- It can result in you always attributing any problems to the syndrome or condition, rather than looking to see whether there is another cause.

Expectations that limit people

Here are some examples of the effects of limiting expectations inappropriately because of a person's syndrome or condition. While you read them, see if any of the situations seem familiar to you.

Examples

Gita

Gita has Down syndrome. Her speech is limited and difficult to make out. Her abilities are often under-estimated because of this, so she is not given the same opportunities as others in the centre, especially tasks that involve more abstract reasoning or reading. Yet at home, she reads the Radio Times, programmes the video and plays a full part in family activities and conversations.

Comment

The expectation is that Gita, because she has Down syndrome, will be less able than others who do not have this syndrome. This is based on a limited expectation of people with Down syndrome and on Gita's speech.

Arnold

Arnold is autistic, and lives in a residential home with other people who have learning disabilities. Expectations of him in social situations are limited, so his anti-social behaviour is generally tolerated – he rushes around, takes things from people and upsets them, and screams loudly when he doesn't get his own way. It's now impossible to take Arnold out anywhere because of his challenging behaviours, so he misses out continually.

Comment

As Arnold has autism (now generally referred to as 'autistic spectrum disorder' because there are many different types), no attempt is made to help him develop any kind of social interaction, apart from negative ones. It is believed that people with autism 'are like that', despite the fact that there are ways of helping Arnold overcome some of his difficulties. He will always have problems with socialisation, but these will become worse if he is left unsupported.

Rona

Rona is 36 years old, has cerebral palsy and lives in a residential home. She spends a lot of her time lying down. She has a small electronic keyboard her mother bought her, which she has taught herself to play. She doesn't speak, but obviously understands a great deal. She responds both to her own language, Tagalog and to English. She is left to her own devices most of the time.

Comment

When you meet Rona, it's obvious that she is intellectually very able. However, because of her very severe physical disabilities, and the way she looks, expectations of her have been low, so her opportunities have been severely restricted.

Activity 9: Limiting expectations

Can you think of one or more examples from your own experience, where expectations of service users have been limited merely because of what people believe or understand about their syndrome or condition? What was the result?

....

....

....

....

Comment

Your example will depend on your own situation and awareness of how other people, and the service in general, respond to people with particular syndromes. It is quite possible that the syndromes and conditions of many service users are not known to you or other workers, unless there is a particular reason for having this information, or if the syndrome or condition is obvious.

We all know about the danger of limiting our expectations just because a person has a learning disability. You might also want to be aware of expectations being limited because of someone's beliefs about a particular syndrome or condition.

☞ *Key points*

Inappropriately limiting your expectations of an individual, because of beliefs about a syndrome or condition, is harmful because:

- it will limit the opportunities you make available to that person
- it might cause you to see problems that don't exist
- you might attribute every problem to the person's syndrome or condition
- it can lead you to look for inabilities rather than abilities
- it can make you expect certain types of behaviours.

Knowing about the effects of a syndrome or condition

There are some occasions when it might be important for you to be aware of the physical, cognitive or behavioural effects of a particular syndrome or condition. It can be useful to know about these effects in the circumstances detailed below, for instance.

Physical effects

- Knowing about various conditions can help you to understand that someone with a particular condition might be more prone to illness or accident in certain situations. You might have to take precautions against this. For example, there are possibilities of spinal injuries from particular sports in people with Down syndrome because of cranio-vertebral instability (problems around the neck area of the spine); people with cerebral palsy are vulnerable to pressure sores.
- It is useful to understand a medical condition that might occur more often in a person with a particular syndrome. For example, heart defects and respiratory problems often occur in people with Down syndrome; there is a possibility of bowel disorders in people with autism.

Cognitive effects

- When tailoring your support to suit the learning needs of an individual, it helps to know as much information as possible about cognitive effects of conditions. For example, it helps to know that someone is likely to have more difficulty understanding spoken language owing to a specific language problem.
- It is important to understand that someone who has a severe physical disability and no speech might have strong cognitive ability and might need alternative or augmentative ways of communicating. This would enable individuals, for example those with cerebral palsy, to make the best of their abilities (like Rona in the example above).
- Realising that people with certain syndromes, for example Down syndrome, are more likely than others to have sensory (sight and hearing) impairments, allows you to support these individuals more effectively.

Behavioural effects

- Understanding the behavioural effects of certain syndromes can enable you to help people overcome challenging behaviours, such as those associated with Fragile X syndrome.
- It is essential to provide appropriate socialisation opportunities for service users with particular syndromes or conditions that limit their interaction with others. For example, with knowledge of the effects of their conditions, you may be able to support people with autistic spectrum disorders or Fragile X syndrome in relating to other people or coping in social situations.

Activity 10: Physical, cognitive and behavioural effects in certain syndromes or conditions

From your own experience, think of two examples where a knowledge of the physical, cognitive or behavioural effects of a syndrome or condition was important in your work – or where it would have been useful if you'd known it at the time.

1 ....

....

2 ....

....

Comment

Did you mention any of the following?

- *Down syndrome – knowing about heart and respiratory problems; the possibility of hearing or visual impairment; the need to check for neck/spinal problems before doing sports.*
- *Autistic spectrum disorders (including Asperger's syndrome) – knowing about difficulties in relating to people, in understanding spoken language and in having the routine upset; challenging behaviours; the possibility of bowel or digestive problems.*
- *Cerebral palsy – knowing that the extent of the physical impairment doesn't indicate the extent of the cognitive impairment; knowing about extraneous movement in athetoid cerebral palsy; the possibility of respiratory problems; the need to avoid pressure sores.*
- *Fragile X syndrome – knowing that males are likely to be more severely affected than females; difficulties in social relationships, problems with attention and concentration; challenging behaviours.*

You may have mentioned other syndromes and conditions not listed here.

☞ *Key points*

Identifying the possible physical, cognitive and behavioural effects of a syndrome or condition can be important in the following circumstances:

- identifying when someone might be more prone to an illness, accident or particular medical condition

- tailoring your support more accurately to suit individual needs
- helping you realise that a particular impairment might mask cognitive ability
- understanding why challenging behaviours occur and how to deal with them.

Researching information and producing a report on the possible effects of a syndrome or condition

There may be occasions when you need to find out more about the effects of a particular syndrome or condition:

- for your own work
- to contribute to training days in your service
- when you're doing further study.

This section is designed to give you guidance on researching information and writing a report.

The more organised you are before you start, the better use you will make of your time.

Planning your report

The *structure* of your report will be similar to the one you used when you were writing a report on causation, as described in the previous section of this workbook. However, the *content* will be different. In this instance, your report will include:

1. A brief introduction stating what the report is about and what the purpose is.
2. A brief description of the syndrome or condition.
3. A description of the *physical effects* on the person.
4. A description of the *cognitive effects* on the person.
5. A description of the *behavioural effects* on the person.
6. Any other *relevant* information (don't include information just because you have discovered it, unless it has a purpose in the report).
7. A paragraph or two about the relevance and/or implications of the cause for people living and/or working with the person, such as how you can help people deal with the effects of the syndrome, what kind of specialist help might be necessary, etc. (This section will be influenced by the reason why you are writing the report.)
8. A description of how you researched the information.

9. Concluding comments – a closing paragraph rounding off the report and making a statement bringing it to a close.
10. Details of the sources of your information, such as leaflets from organisations, book references and website addresses.
11. Names and addresses of organisations, if appropriate.

Once you've planned your report, it's time to get started on the research.

Researching the information

Sources

You have several sources, most of which are listed in the previous section. To remind you, they are:

* libraries
* support groups and organisations dealing with the syndrome or condition
* other specialist organisations
* websites.

Getting the information

This is the stage where good planning really pays off. You should have a fairly clear idea of what you are looking for. Here are some tips, some of which will be familiar to you.

Some tips for library research

* Use the computer to help you identify the best sources. If you don't know how, ask the librarian. Have your key words ready, for example Down syndrome, learning disabilities.
* Use skimming and scanning techniques with books and journals, ie, don't start by reading the whole book from cover to cover; instead, read through the contents list, chapter headings and summaries or conclusions at the end of chapters. Then select the parts that are of most use and read these more thoroughly.
* Ask for help if you get stuck – don't waste time.
* Use up-to-date sources.

Some tips for getting information from organisations

* Be clear in your requests. Explain what you are doing and be precise about the information you want, but don't write a long letter as nobody will have time to read it – a couple of paragraphs are enough.
* Offer to pay for postage.
* If the organisation looks for the information for you specially, ring or write to thank them. This is not necessary if it is a large organisation which has ready prepared material which gets sent out to all enquirers.

Some tips for using websites

- If you are not used to the internet, get someone to show you how to use it and practise. It's very easy to use once you get over your fear.
- Be as precise as possible with your key words when you are searching.
- Be selective in the websites you use. Don't opt for the first one you come across and don't use one that has too much jargon or is too technical – if you can't understand it, don't use it.

Some tips for writing your report

- Look back to your plan and use it to help you structure your report.
- Be selective in the information you use. Don't just copy the words from the book or leaflet – put it into your own words. Don't give unnecessary detail.
- Be as precise as possible. Aim to keep your report short and to the point.
- Write the first draft and then leave it. Come back to it a few days later and improve it.
- Read it aloud to yourself to hear the 'flow'.
- Write as many drafts as you want until you are satisfied.

Some tips on explaining how you researched the information

- Be factual – say exactly what you did and how.
- Explain why you chose these sources and methods of working.
- Don't go into too much detail.
- Explain what worked well and what was not effective.

Addresses and references

At the end of your report include:

- the names and addresses of the organisations you contacted, with telephone numbers, fax numbers and e-mail addresses where they have one.
- a list of website addresses.
- book references, in the example formats shown below.

If the whole book is written by one or more authors:

Name of author(s), date, title of book in italics, place of publication, publisher.

For example:
Hughes, J. (1999) *Research for Beginners*. Glasgow: Blackie and Sons.

If the different chapters were written by different people and the book has an overall editor (named on the cover):

Name of person who wrote the chapter you used, date of book, title of chapter, name(s) of editor, book title in italics, place of publication, publisher.

For example:
Mulligan, B. (2000) Career Advancement. In Heggarty, R. (Ed.) *Getting Back to Work*. Liverpool: Ivanhoe Publishers.

If you used a journal article:

Name of person who wrote the article, date, title of article, name of journal in italics, volume number, page numbers.

For example:
Brodie, S. (2001) Lifelong Learning. *British Journal of Continuing Education*, 80, 167-189.

The role of support and information groups

You'll have noticed in several places the mention of *support groups*. You'll probably have had contact with at least some of these kinds of groups in relation to your work or other responsibilities. Two of the best known are Mencap, in England, Wales and Scotland, and Enable, in Scotland. Support groups serve many purposes, but their primary role is to provide *support* especially to families and people with learning disabilities themselves.

Support groups can be local, national or international. Most rely to a large extent on fund-raising, but might also have access to government funding, such as grants from the NHS or Social Services (England, Northern Ireland and Wales) or Social Work Department (Scotland). They might also be eligible for funding from UK charitable bodies such as the National Lottery, or Children in Need. Some support groups, especially those which campaign on important issues relating to people with learning disabilities, steer clear of government funding in order to retain their independence and fight for particular rights.

Some groups have been formed merely for the purpose of providing information and this is their only role, mainly because they do not have the resources to do otherwise. An example might be a local helpline which will answer queries and direct enquirers to other groups, provide details of benefit systems or supply information leaflets.

Most groups, however, combine these two roles of providing information and providing support. They might, for example:

- have parent counselling or support services where parents with older children support new parents of children with learning disability;
- run activities for the whole family;

- provide information for parents, professionals and people with learning disabilities about all aspects, or particular aspects of learning disabilities;
- provide information and support about all types of learning disability, or focus only on one type, eg, Mencap and Enable are examples of the first, while the National Autistic Society is an example of the second;
- provide services as well as more informal support, eg, different kinds of supported housing; employment schemes.

In your home area, you are likely to have branches of national organisations as well as smaller local groups, most probably started by local people in response to a gap in support services. Think about this by doing the next activity.

Activity 11: Support groups

Make a list of the support/information groups you are aware of in your own locality.

....

....

....

....

....

....

....

Choose two of these groups which you know well. For each group, describe how they benefit service users with learning disabilities, families and other carers, professionals.

Comment

Did you mention any of the following benefits:

For service users:

- *obtaining information about what benefits are available to them*
- *helping them deal with problems which have arisen*

- *providing a listening ear and/or advice*
- *putting them in touch with people in similar situations*
- *providing information on courses and other training activities*
- *helping them find out about leisure activities*
- *helping with specific issues, such as employment or housing*
- *helping in times of problems with authorities, such as police.*

For family and other carers:

- *benefits advice*
- *information and support with respite care*
- *support from other families and carers*
- *information about syndromes and conditions*
- *information on courses and other training activities*
- *assistance with problems with statutory bodies, such as the local authority which provides services.*

Professionals:

- *information on courses and other training activities*
- *information about syndromes and conditions*
- *information about other organisations*
- *help with sources of funding for particular activities*
- *advice with particular problems.*

You probably included others. Support groups engage in a wide variety of activities, often on limited funding and with the help of reliable volunteers. It is important to bear this in mind when you approach them for advice, information or assistance.

☞ *Key points*

Support/information groups benefit service users, carers and professionals by:

- providing accurate and up-to-date information about all aspects of learning disabilities
- acting as a liaison between individuals and other groups, either statutory or voluntary
- providing activities or services
- helping with particular problems.

Support/information groups might deal with the whole range of learning disabilities or might focus on just one type of learning disability.

From your own experience

You are likely to have experienced situations in which other people's attitudes and behaviour towards people with learning disabilities really angered you and probably the people with learning disabilities involved in the incident. Mistaken ideas and lack of understanding about learning disabilities are rife in our society. It is clear that far too many people see the disability, not the person. As someone who works with people with learning disabilities, you are in a good position to help overcome this problem.

This section has focused a lot on the effects of particular syndromes and conditions and the relevance of this kind of knowledge for your work. However, we know that it's the *person* who counts, not the disability. It is our responsibility to promote this understanding. In the final section of this workbook we explore this issue in greater depth.

The disabling effects of society's response to learning disabilities

The disabling effects of society's response to learning disabilities

Introduction

We've covered a lot of ground in this workbook. It's appropriate now to return to the heart of the matter – the way in which the people we work with are disabled much more by society than by their learning disability.

In this final section I explore:

- the way in which disability is socially constructed
- labelling, stigma and stereotyping
- the difference between the social model of disability and the medical model of disability
- the disabling effects of society's response to learning disability
- philosophies aimed at conteracting the disabling effects of society's response to learning disabilities
- practical ways of working against these disabling effects within society.

The social construction of disability

In section three, when discussing how society's attitudes to learning disability are shaped to a large extent by the causes of the disability, I mentioned the fact that many people within our society have a concept of something they believe to be 'normality'. The way in which society is constructed is based on this ill-informed and restricted concept of what is and isn't 'normal'.

There are many people who don't fit this picture of what society considers 'normal', people with learning disabilities amongst them. As a result of this, people with learning disabilities experience the kinds of judgemental and disempowering attitudes and responses which were discussed in section 1: exclusion, segregation, lack of opportunity, social control and lack of choice.

This can be illustrated by Sally's story.

Sally's story

Sally lives in a council flat on the fifth floor of a tower block. She took over the tenancy when her father died three years ago. She has cerebral palsy and walks with the help of two sticks, although this is difficult for her, time consuming and very tiring. She has a wheelchair, but cannot get it into the bedroom, bathroom or kitchen as the doors are too narrow.

She has been offered the help of a carer three days a week but has turned this down as she prefers to do things for herself and keep her privacy. Sally has a mild learning disability. She would like to get a job, but there is no possibility of that at present, so she has been offered a place in an adult training centre, which she has turned down. She went once and hated it as there was very little going on which she felt suited her needs or abilities.

The lifts in the tower block are often out of action, so, even when she does feel able to go out, it isn't always possible.

We could analyse Sally's story like this:

Sally has a physical disability. Because of this she can hardly walk. She's more or less wheelchair bound. She gets exhausted very easily because her disability makes it difficult for her to look after herself. She's also got a learning disability which makes it difficult for her to learn. It's unrealistic for her to think about getting a job. She will have to compete with 'able-bodied' 'intellectually normal' people if she wants to get a job, so there's little chance of her getting one. It's difficult even for normal people to get jobs in her area. She probably hasn't been able to learn the skills she needs to get a job, because of her learning disability. She probably doesn't even understand what a job of work involves. Besides, she's probably not up to it physically.

She won't cooperate with the people who are trying to help her. She won't let a carer in, even though this would save her doing everything for herself, and stop her wasting time and getting exhausted. It'd be better for her. Also, she can't use her wheelchair in the flat, so what's the point of having it there? Perhaps she could keep it in somebody's garage. If she let a carer look after her, this person could get her dressed and then take her out – providing the lifts were working, of course. If they weren't she'd have to stay at home because she can't walk down the stairs like other people. She won't go to the day centre, even though it's for people like her, so once again she's uncooperative. Her life would be much better if only she'd take what is on offer and listen to people who only want to help her. She won't listen to reason – thinks she knows best.

From this analysis we can see that:

- All the problems are attributed to Sally's physical and learning impairments
- Sally is seen as uncooperative because she won't do what she's expected to do or take the kind of services and support which are available

- She's expected to have her life organised and run by other people who know better than she does;
- Compared to 'normal' people, she is seen as not at all able, so shouldn't expect to have the same opportunities as them.

However, there is another way of looking at it, one which is much more acceptable. This is generally referred to as the *social model of disability*.

The social model of disability
In this context, we would analyse Sally's situation like this:

- Sally does have a physical impairment and has difficulty walking
- Sally does have a learning disability and probably takes longer to learn some things than many other people
- Sally's problems, however, are due to other things:
  - ⇨ The fact that she lives in a tower block with lifts that often don't work (these lifts will also cause problems for other people in the building – mothers with young children and older people, for example, not to mention those who live on the fifteenth floor)
  - ⇨ The fact that the doors to her bathroom, bedroom and kitchen are not wide enough for her wheelchair
  - ⇨ The fact that she is being described according to what are considered her 'deficits', rather than as a unique human being with both strengths and needs, like the rest of us
  - ⇨ The fact that the kinds of services and support available to her are totally unsuitable and ignore her own wishes and aspirations
  - ⇨ The fact that the range of options available is very restricted
  - ⇨ The fact that she is expected to be dependent on someone else for very private and personal areas of her life
  - ⇨ The fact that she is expected to be grateful for what is available
  - ⇨ The fact that she is seen as inferior to other people and not entitled to the same rights as they have.

Even the words that are used are oppressive and discriminatory, eg, 'wheelchair *bound*', 'uncooperative'.

By thinking about her situation in this way, we can begin to see where the real problem lies – not within Sally, but within our society, the one which we have designed and created. This is the nub of the problem. The society we have created is designed not for the range of diversity which exists within humanity, but for only a restricted proportion of humanity. Anyone who doesn't conform to the idea of 'normality' mentioned above, is perceived as *different* in negative terms. This includes many people: minority ethnic groups, people with physical or sensory impairments, people with mental health problems, people who are very poor, people who sleep on the streets, children who don't fit into the education system – and people with learning disabilities.

The social model of disability is based on the fact that it is not their impairment which *disables* people, but the way in which society has been *socially constructed* to suit some people and not others. This understanding of disability does not ignore or deny the impairment – which is an important aspect of the individual – but sees it as only one characteristic. What is most important is that we all share a common humanity and all have the same rights.

Therefore, society disables people through:

* The built environment, in which we have created physical barriers, such as Sally's tower block and the doors in her flat which aren't wide enough
* The discrimination and oppression which people face within society
* The lack of equality of opportunity, eg, you and I have a range of options from which to choose, but Sally has to put up with what is available for 'people like her'
* The negative beliefs and attitudes of other people
* The denial of equal rights.

When we analyse Sally's situation according to the social model of disability, we can see that the problem lies not within Sally, but within society. Let us think in a bit more detail how this happens.

The *social construction* of learning disability leads to prejudice, discrimination and oppression. In real life, this means that:

* People with learning disabilities are marked out as *different* from other people in society, ie, as inferior
* They are *excluded* from many aspects of life that other people have access to
* They have many fewer opportunities in all aspects of life than other people have
* They are segregated within society

as we can see from Sally's story.

This discrimination and oppression operates in all areas of life: education, employment, health, housing, leisure and community participation. Because people are denied the opportunities they should rightly be able to access, they have fewer opportunities to mix with other people and to learn the skills they require to control the different dimensions of their own lives.

There are three important concepts you need to be familiar with in relation to the social construction of disability: *labelling, social stigma* and *stereotyping*.

You have probably come across these words in your work, so it is worth checking that you fully understand what they mean.

Labelling
Every one of us carries certain labels:

* Family labels: mother, sister, grandfather, son
* Labels about the way in which we are categorised by the institutions in society: patient, student, teacher, administrator, client, claimant
* Labels which define the work we do: bus driver, architect, nurse, shopkeeper, civil servant.

Labels are useful, both as shorthand, and as ways of describing our relationship to different institutions and organisations within society. As a customer, I shop, and expect certain levels of service. As a patient I see a doctor, or have an operation. As a student, I study.

Labels carry values and confer an *identity* on us. When this identity is positive, we are *socially valued* within society. Think, for example, of the social status of doctors, judges and politicians.

But labels can also be derogatory and damaging: loony, down-and-out, nutter, pervert, for example. Not labels that anyone would want to own.

Labelling, in our context, means ascribing to people with learning disabilities a negative label based only on one of their characteristics: their intellectual impairment (the fact that they have a learning disability.) This label ignores the humanity we all share and the fact that the learning disability is only one aspect of someone's identity. The label, in society's eyes, *becomes* the person's identity and everything about them is perceived through this negative definition of who and what they are.

This negative label has several effects:

* It *devalues* people with learning disabilities within society
* It identifies them as *deviant* or different
* It makes it permissible to treat them in ways we would not treat other human beings
* It allows us to deny them their full human rights.

In addition to being labelled with the term *learning disabilities*, people are also labelled in terms of their syndrome or condition, eg, a Downs girl, the cp man, and in other devaluing terms, eg, crazy, mental, retarded, not right in the head, spastic. You will probably have heard many other derogatory labels in the course of your work or other experience.

The label is further reinforced by the actions of society in excluding and segregating people – in special schools, separate adult services and hospitals, for example, and in making it difficult for them to participate in mainstream activities.

Social stigma

Like labelling, social stigma is based on the concept of *deviance* or difference. Within society, people are valued differently according to their social status. There is no valid reason for this. It is something which we ourselves have created. If we were to go back to the stone age, the people who would be most highly valued within society would likely be the men who can run fastest and hunt best.

Not surprisingly, the people with the most power and influence – usually referred to as the *dominant group* – are the ones who have the greatest say in which values are and aren't desirable within a society.

In our society, as a general rule, we base our judgement of people on:

* Their social standing within their community
* The job they do
* The amount of money they earn
* The people they mix with
* The kind of accent they have
* Their level of education
* The colour of their skin.

You will see that people with learning disabilities are much more likely to be *socially devalued* if judged against these criteria, than socially valued.

Judging people with learning disabilities in this negative way is generally referred to as ascribing *social stigma*. Within our society, people who do not conform to certain criteria are stigmatised or *marked out as different*.

Stereotyping

The third concept relevant to this discussion of the social construction of disability is that of *stereotyping*. This refers to the tendency to group people together according to a particular label, and ascribe certain negative characteristics to everyone who belongs to that group. Thus, everyone who is labelled as having learning disabilities is perceived within society in a negative way: as helpless, dependent and pitiful, for example.

People are also stereotyped according to particular syndromes or conditions. For example:

- People with autism have photographic memories and are good at drawing
- People with Down syndrome are affectionate and love music
- Men with mild learning disabilities are over-sexed
- Blind people have extra special hearing to make up for the fact that they can't see.

An understanding of labelling, social stigma and stereotyping is useful in helping us identify the way in which learning disability is constructed within society, and the effects this has on people with learning disability.

We can also develop a better understanding of the social construction of disability if we compare the *social model of disability* with the *medical model of disability*.

The differences between the social model of disability and the medical model of disability

The social model of disability, identified and developed by disabled people themselves, mainly those with physical or sensory impairment, is discussed above in relation to Sally's story. But the model of disability which has been most prevalent until fairly recently, is the other one, the first one applied to Sally's situation. This is known as the medical model of disability. The major difference between the two models are that the social model sees people as disabled by *society* – which, you will remember, is socially constructed by the dominant group – whereas the medical model sees the disability as residing within *the person* herself and as the result of her impairment. We can identify other differences in the two models as outlined below.

The medical model	*The social model*
The disability arises from the individual's impairment	The person is disabled by the social construction of society
The person cannot take part in 'normal' activities in society because he is disabled, eg, cannot walk, or learn easily, or hear, or see	Society creates physical, political, attitudinal and social barriers which exclude a large number of people who have impairments
Stresses the 'difference' or deviance of people who do not fit into narrowly designed criteria	Stresses the diversity within humankind
Focuses on *in*capacities, ie, what a person cannot do	Focuses on people's capacities
Expects disabled people to conform to the role ascribed to them, ie, dependent, pitiful, incomplete	Recognises the individuality and humanity of everyone

From this comparison, you can see how the two models, applied above to Sally's story, result in two very different pictures:

- the medical model, where she is dependent and pathetic, not in control of her own life and expected to cooperate and be grateful for whatever is offered to her, even if this is vastly inferior to what is available to non-disabled people
- her own view of herself, which is more like the social model, where she is in control and entitled to the same opportunities as other people.

You can also see that the problem arises because the medical model is being applied in her situation, rather than the social model.

☞ *Key points*

The social model of disability identifies disability as a social construct which arises because of the way in which society disables people with impairments by discrimination, oppression and the denial of full human rights.

The social construction of disability subjects people with learning disabilities to labelling, social stigma and stereotyping.

Labelling involves ascribing to people with learning disabilities a negative and devalued identity and social role based solely on the fact of their intellectual impairment.

Social stigma involves identifying people with learning disabilities as socially deviant and different from other people within society.

Stereotyping in this context refers to ascribing to people with learning disabilities certain negative characteristics thought by society at large to be associated with learning disability.

The differences between the social model of disability and the medical model of disability are:

- that the social model identifies disability as socially constructed by society because of discrimination and oppression; whereas the medical model sees disability as a direct result of an individual's own impairment

- the social model focuses on capacity; the medical model focuses on incapacity
- the social model recognises the diversity of humankind and the rights of everyone to freedom, equality of opportunity and control over their own lives; the medical model sees people with impairments as people who are less than whole, abnormal and incapacitated when compared with 'normal' people.

Think about all of this in relation to your own experience by doing the next activity.

Activity 12 : Labelling, stigma and stereotyping

Think about two people with learning disabilities who are known to you. Think about the way in which the social model of disability applies to the lives of these two people. Do this by describing:

- *the ways in which labelling, stigma and stereotyping applies to them*
- *the disabling effects of society in the different areas of their lives, eg, barriers to living an ordinary life in the community, any physical barriers they experience, attitudinal barriers, barriers in work and leisure lives, barriers in relationships.*

List below three ways that labelling, stigma and stereotyping might apply to the two people:

1

2

3

List below three ways that the disabling effects of society might affect their lives:

1 ....

....

2 ....

....

3 ....

....

Comment

Your own examples will be specific to your situation. Look back through the contents of this section to make sure you have covered all the ways in which these two people are disabled by the way in which society is socially constructed.

....

The implications of the social construction of disability for people with learning disabilities

Because society labels people with learning disability as 'different' and devalues them by stigmatising and stereotyping, they are discriminated against in all areas of life. This means that:

- they do not have access to the same opportunities for education, work, housing, employment and leisure as people who are not disabled by society
- they are excluded from many mainstream areas of life
- they are segregated within society
- they are seen as a homogeneous group all with the same needs and aspirations, and their individuality is denied
- they are expected to behave in a certain way, eg, as dependent, submissive, grateful for what they are given.

This perception of people with learning disabilities has shaped the kinds of support and facilities that are made available to them and which they are expected to make use of. This has included:

- segregated schooling – special schools, where they are kept apart from other children

- segregated adult services where they can be with people 'of their own kind'
- segregated accommodation such as hospitals, hostels and special housing
- 'therapeutic' activities, eg, you and I might garden or go trampolining – people with learning disabilities take part in horticultural therapy or rebound therapy.

It has also resulted in different expectations of them and constraints upon them, some of which were discussed in section two: denial of their rights to form relationships, get married and have children, for example. These are discussed in more detail below.

Negative attitudes and barriers to equal opportunities

- The implication that, because of their disability, people are unable to speak for themselves and have nothing worthwhile to say.
- Stigmatised identities, such as 'eternal children', 'sexually promiscuous', 'threatening', etc.
- Lack of social status within society and no political voice, so their opinions are generally invisible.
- Disablist language which is used to describe and refer to people, such as 'mental age', 'suffering from', 'a victim of', etc. This kind of language portrays people with learning disabilities as tragic, dependent and pitiful; they are perceived as of less value than others.
- The images of learning disability as portrayed in the media.
- Disabling policies, such as having to identify what you are incapable of in order to get benefits from the state.
- Segregated facilities in all areas of life.

Barriers to mainstream education

- Children with learning disabilities do not, on the whole, have access to the same education as other children.
- Schools are not designed or equipped to respond to the needs of all children.

Barriers to employment

- Low paid and low skilled jobs.
- Discrimination within the labour market.
- Discriminatory attitudes and behaviours of employers.
- The benefit system is stacked against people being able to work.

Barriers to information

- The way in which information is presented also makes it inaccessible to people with learning disabilities, both because of vocabulary and of writing style.
- People with learning disabilities are seldom consulted when information is being compiled. Therefore, most written information takes no account of

their perceptions or opinions. This further removes from them control of their own lives.

Barriers to mainstream leisure activities

- The physical environment excludes people with additional disabilities such as mobility difficulties.
- Leisure activities are expensive; people with disabilities are poor.
- There is little encouragement for people with learning disabilities to join mainstream leisure activities; most of their leisure pursuits are segregated ones.

Barriers to living independently in their own homes

- Poverty, as a result of having no job, or a poorly paid job.
- Other people controlling their lives.
- Lack of opportunity for developing an independent lifestyle.
- Lack of support for many which would enable them to live independently.

☞ *Key points*

The implications of the social construction of disability for people with learning disabilities are:

- a denial of their rights as human beings
- lack of choice
- lack of equality of opportunity with other people in society
- barriers to participation in mainstream society
- lack of control over their own lives.

Philosophies aimed at counteracting the disabling effects of society's response to learning disability

The task of helping people overcome the disabling effects they encounter within society is an enormous one if we take a broad view. However, we have to remember that society is *you and me,* and other people like us. So, if we bring the problems back to a personal level, we can begin to see some of the ways in which we can work against disabling attitudes, beliefs and practices.

Think about this by doing this activity, which asks you to reflect on your own experience.

Activity 13: Working against disabling responses

A. Have you ever done any of the following?   *Yes*   *No*

*Tried to help someone using disablist language
understand that they are being disablist.*   ☐   ☐

*Corrected someone's mistaken understanding
about people with learning disabilities.*   ☐   ☐

*Objected to the language used about people
with learning disabilities.*   ☐   ☐

*Written or phoned about discrimination
in newspaper, radio or television.*   ☐   ☐

*Objected to the way people with learning
disabilities were written about in policy
or planning documents.*   ☐   ☐

*Objected to the fact that no-one with learning
disabilities was present at a meeting or
discussion about issues concerning them.*   ☐   ☐

*Explained about learning disabilities to a
relative, friend or acquaintance.*   ☐   ☐

*Been involved in any support or
advocacy work with people with
learning disabilities in your own time.*   ☐   ☐

B. In your work, do you do any of the following?   *Yes*   *No*

Discuss people's rights with them.   ☐   ☐

*Discuss with them any discrimination
they've encountered and how they might deal
with it.*   ☐   ☐

*Discuss important issues such as
employment, relationships, etc.*   ☐   ☐

*Support people in ordinary community
activities, either as individuals, or in pairs.*   ☐   ☐

C. In your work, do you do the following?   *Yes*   *No*

Recognise, respect and uphold the
adult status of service users.   ☐   ☐

Provide age-appropriate activities.   ☐   ☐

Involve people in planning and decision-making.   ☐   ☐

Work towards inclusion in mainstream
community activities for service users.   ☐   ☐

If appropriate, help service users develop the
skills they need to advocate for themselves.   ☐   ☐

If appropriate, help them develop the skills they
need to represent the views of other service users.   ☐   ☐

Comment

If you said 'yes' to any of the items in A or B, which you almost certainly did, then you are already working against the disabling effects of society towards people with learning disabilities. You're already part of their struggle against inequality. The more times you ticked 'yes', the more active you are in this struggle. You could probably add many more to the list.

If you couldn't answer 'yes' to anything, that may be because of the type of work you do. You probably do other things to combat 'disablism'.

In C, your answers will depend on the type of work you do and the people you work with. For example, if the service users all have profound and complex learning disabilities, the item about representing others won't apply.

Obviously, there are limits to your ability to make major changes in the service in which you work. But major change is not always what's required. Sometimes *incremental* change, that is change that happens bit by bit, is more powerful. There is *always* something we can all do, no matter how small. Sometimes this will be in the workplace, sometimes in the wider world. Some examples are listed here. Could you do any of these things?

- Start with yourself. Look at what you do and how you do it. How are you currently helping service users become more empowered? Could you do more of this? What are you doing that stops people becoming empowered, for example making decisions for them, not encouraging enough independence? How can you change this?

- Are service users partners in planning, policy-making and decision-making in your service? How could you work towards this? Who could help?
- Are there other responsibilities people could take on in the service? Could you discuss this with managers?
- How innovative is your service in relation to housing and employment (if you are involved in these areas)? Are there more creative things you could try? Do the same sorts of things happen year after year?
- Are you doing really innovative things that could be shared with other people and other services? How could you share these innovative practices?
- What is the best thing your service does to work against disabling attitudes and practices in society? How can you share this with other services?
- What is the worst thing about your service in relation to the issues discussed in this section? How can you change this or persuade other people to change it?

You will be able to add to this list from your own experience and knowledge.

The philosophies aimed at counteracting the disabling effects of society's response to learning disabilities

Many of the practices we use today are embedded in philosophies which have influenced the development of services over the last forty years. A knowledge of these philosophies will help you understand what has shaped the way we think about learning disability in the present day and why services have developed in the way they have done. In the final part of this section, I focus on some of these philosophies:

- Normalisation
- Social role valorisation
- Ordinary life principles
- Empowerment
- Social inclusion.

Normalisation

Normalisation originated in Scandinavia in the late 1950s, and influenced services in Denmark and Sweden throughout the 1960s. Wolfensberger developed it in the USA in the 1970s and from there it was transported to the UK. Normalisation was originally concerned with making available to people with learning disabilities lifestyles which are as close as possible to the patterns of mainstream life. The role of services was to make this happen for service users.

Social role valorisation

In 1983, Wolfensberger developed his ideas further and redefined normalisation as *social role valorisation* (SRV for short). SRV was based on the premise that people who are labelled as having 'learning disabilities' have devalued social roles within our society. These devalued roles lead to discrimination, exclusion and segregation. The role of services is to reverse this state of affairs and help people gain access to valued experiences in society. When people are grouped together in service settings according to their impairment, they are further stigmatised and the process of devaluation and segregation is compounded.

Being devalued within society not only influences society's perceptions and responses to people with learning disabilities, but also affects the way in which people perceive and value themselves. We must therefore change this situation for people who have been negatively valued and enable them to become culturally valued. Normalisation and SRV require not only changes in the services we provide for people, but also the way in which people perceive or *value* themselves and in the attitudes within society.

Normalisation and, later, SRV, had a considerable influence on service development in the UK in the 1970s and 1980s, but has also attracted much criticism. The main criticisms have been:

- That the focus is on changing people rather than challenging unequal social structures within society
- That the *valued lifestyle* espoused by the philosophy is one which takes no account of cultural and social diversity, ie, it is the culture of the dominant people within society and excludes many who do not belong to this group
- That the *culturally valued roles* which are central to the philosophy are also based on the values of the dominant group within society and take no account of gender, individuality, or cultural, ethnic or economic diversity
- That people are further stigmatised because their learning disability is seen as an undesirable aspect of their identity
- That it is a service led movement and that the control remains in the hands of professionals.

Despite these criticisms, normalisation and SRV were instrumental in bringing the rights of people with learning disabilities to the fore and in promoting the closure of institutions.

Ordinary Life Principles

Normalisation also had an influence on another development in the UK: that of the *Ordinary Life* movement, as set out in the King's Fund document *An Ordinary Life,* published in 1980. The Ordinary Life movement prioritised ordinary housing for people with learning disabilities and community membership, ie, the use of ordinary community facilities and services.

As part of this development, John O'Brien's *Five Accomplishments* identified particular service goals:

- Community presence – the right to experience a wide range of ordinary activities in ordinary community settings
- Community participation – the right to experience a wide range of relationships with other people in the community
- Choice – maximum opportunities for choice in all areas of life
- Competence – opportunities for individuals to develop their own strengths, skills and interests in community settings
- Respect – enhancing the images of people with learning disabilities through presenting positive images.

Ordinary life principles had a strong influence on many of the services which were being developed during that period, especially those seeking alternatives to the large long-stay institutions.

Here again, you can see that the greatest emphasis is on *services,* and on the role of the professionals, rather than on the inequality which exists within the structures of society.

Empowerment

The term *empowerment* is very common nowadays, but it emerged only relatively recently as a philosophy in relation to people with learning disabilities. Empowerment moves away from the emphasis mentioned above on services and the role of professionals, and focuses more directly on the way in which power is unevenly distributed in society. Anya Souza expresses her view of the disempowerment which people with learning disabilities face:

'It takes a lot of courage and strength to fight against people who have the power to define who you are. People who think they can define you also assume they can tell you what your rights are and, because of who they think you are, specify what you should do with your life. They don't specify this by telling you what to do with your life only. It's worse than that. They put you in situations where there are only a limited range of things you can do with your life.' (p.4)

Souza, A. (with Ramcharan, P) (1997) Everything You Ever Wanted to Know About Down's Syndrome but Never Bothered to Ask, in Ramcharan, P. et al, *Empowerment in Everyday Life: Learning Disability,* London: Jessica Kingsley.

From this statement, you will see that it is not only *people* who are responsible for disempowering those with learning disabilities, but also the *structures* within society: special schools which restrict opportunity, segregate children and further stigmatise them; restricted opportunities for living in ordinary houses and getting real jobs; social welfare systems, laws and policies which focus on *in*capacity; segregated adult services. Add to this the perceptions and attitudes which are perpetuated by the segregation and exclusion people with learning disabilities experience.

Empowerment is undoubtedly a potentially potent philosophy, but is not without its critics. For example:

- That not enough research or analysis of the concept of empowerment has been undertaken, and that it remains too abstract, which makes it impossible to determine whether or not people have become empowered;
- That, like other philosophies, the concept has been hijacked by professionals, who can shape it to suit their own ends and describe whatever they are doing in terms of empowerment;
- That empowerment has been effective at the individual level, but not more widely, so that it hasn't in fact, challenged or changed any of the disempowering structures within society.

Another problem is that professionals often talk about *empowering* people with learning disabilities, whereas the only person who can empower someone is the individual herself. What professional, and other supporters can do, is to help people with learning disabilities gain access to opportunities through which they will become empowered.

There is also an argument that empowerment can only be achieved by collective action and that this will only be possible for those people with learning disabilities who have the ability to represent themselves and other people. This excludes people with more severe intellectual impairment. However, their interests might also be served through the use of independent advocates for those people who cannot represent their own interests.

The self advocacy movement draws strongly upon the philosophy of empowerment.

Social inclusion

This is the most recent philosophy to come to the fore, although it has been present in various forms for some time. Social inclusion has figured prominently in government policy over recent years, in relation to various groups of people in society who experience social *exclusion*. Social exclusion happens to different groups of people within society in many different ways: through poverty, lack of appropriate education, alienation from the dominant culture, ethnicity and, of course, disability. Because society is designed to maintain and perpetuate the interests of the dominant group, anyone who doesn't belong to this group is marginalized.

Social *inclusion* is the antidote to social exclusion. Social inclusion can be effected by identifying the cause of the exclusion and developing ways of combating it. This can be done through:

- Recognising the diversity which exists within our society and taking account of it in policy making
- Ensuring that information is made available to socially excluded groups in accessible formats, eg, different ethnic languages, sign language, Braille, simplified formats, picture formats, audio and videotape
- Listening to the views, problems and aspirations of marginalized groups
- Facilitating the participation of marginalized groups in decision making and policy making
- Recognising and upholding the rights of excluded people and enabling them to exercise these rights.

Links between these philosophies and your own work

Several aspects of these philosophies probably struck a chord with you in relation to your own work. We have arrived at the stage we are at today because of their influence. Things like:

- Recognising and promoting the rights of people with learning disabilities to ordinary lifestyles, community participation and control over their own lives (normalisation, SRV, ordinary life principles, empowerment)
- Working with people to combat the prejudice and discrimination they face within society, by enabling them to speak out and challenge situations from which they are excluded (social inclusion, empowerment)
- Helping people to ensure that their needs and aspirations are taken account of in policy and planning (social inclusion, empowerment)
- Supporting people in putting their views across, through self advocacy, for example (empowerment)
- Helping people develop the skills they need to live their desired lifestyles in the community (normalisation, SRV, ordinary life principles)
- Supporting people in making choices and decisions and gaining more control over their own lives (normalisation, SRV, ordinary life principles, empowerment).

This is a general list – you should be able to make it more specific to your own circumstances by relating the philosophies discussed to your own work situation. Do this in the next activity.

Activity 14: Examples from personal experience

Think of one service user who you work with regularly.

Give two examples of ways in which you have attempted to reduce the disabling effects of society's responses to learning disability in relation to this person. (Activity 11 above might give you some ideas to get you started.)

1

2

Now re-read the philosophies outlined above and identify the ones which underpin the approach you used in each of your two examples. Explain how these philosophies relate to what you did. Now evaluate the effectiveness of your actions by describing:

- *What worked well and why you think it worked*
- *What didn't work so well and why you think it didn't work*
- *What you would do differently next time and why (include any philosophies you didn't use this time which might be helpful next time).*

☞ *Key points*

We can combat the disabling effects of society's response to learning disabilities in the following ways:	*Combat by:*
Exclusion and marginalisation of people with learning disabilities	Working towards full inclusion
Inequality and lack of opportunity	Challenging disabling systems, policies and practices
Denial of their rights as fully participating citizens	Helping people with learning disabilities to become empowered and to advocate for themselves and others

Our approaches to working with people with learning disabilities in the present day have been influenced by the philosophies of normalisation, social role valorisation, ordinary life principles, empowerment and social inclusion.

Normalisation and social role valorisation are based on the rights of people with learning disabilities to lead culturally valued lifestyles within society.

Ordinary life principles relate to the rights of people with learning disabilities to live in ordinary houses and be full members of their communities.

Empowerment refers to the need for the equalisation of power within society and the rights of people with learning disabilities to have autonomy, choice, self determination and control over their own lives.

Social inclusion involves changing society to take account of diversity and enabling socially marginalized groups of people to have access to the same rights and opportunities as everyone else within society.

Comments on the disabling effects of society's response from the A&S Group

'You try to explain things. You lose your temper. It's how people talk. They keep on at you for something.'

'It's another way. Bullying and humouring us. The police say everything's all right – they're not being honest. There's an awful long way to go. They've never been honest. They're always right. We can't argue.'

'Somebody with Down's syndrome wanted an operation but she's not getting a heart transplant because she's got Down's syndrome.'

'I went to both kinds of school. I can look at it two ways. First school had a unit. They told my parents your son's a bit slow – good they were doing something about it. They advised my parents about special school. I left my brother and sister behind. Not the most pleasant way. I drew strength from my brother and sister. I sometimes got bullied in the playground. Basically we

need full integration. We can slowly get together but we still need special schools. It's a half-way point. We could get more help. The teachers were trained. The mainstream teachers don't get trained to help people like me. They should work beside teachers in a special school to get trained.'

'The teacher should make the class aware of the disabled person in the classroom. He's no different from anybody else. They should tell other children about learning disabilities: "Anne's no better, you're no better. Anne's a wee bit slow." Then they know what's the weakness. They will understand better if they know.'

'Disabled people have a right to be in the same place as everyone else, treated like everyone else, not just thrown away to one side. We've a right to be heard.'

Section 6:
Resources

Resources

You may find it helpful to look at one or two of the following books or websites or contact the organisations for more information.

Publications

An Ordinary Life: Comprehensive locally-based residential services for mentally handicapped people (1980) London, Kings Fund Publications.

Atkinson, D. et al. (1997) *Forgotten Lives: Exploring the History of Learning Disability* Kidderminster, BILD.

Atkinson, D. et al. (2000) *Good Times, Bad Times: Women with Learning Difficulties Telling their Stories* Kidderminster, BILD.

Booth, T., Booth, W. (1998) *Growing up with parents who have learning difficulties*, London, Routledge.

Department of Health (2001) *Valuing People: A new strategy for Learning Disability for the 21st Century* London, The Stationery Office.

Emerson, E. et al. (2000) *Learning Disabilities: the Fundamental Facts* London, The Foundation for People with Learning Disabilities.

Fraser, W. et al. (1998) Hallas': *The Care of People with Intellectual Disabilities* London, Butterworth Heinemann.

Hughes, A. and Coombs, P. (2001) *Easy Guide to the Human Rights Act 1998: Implications for people with Learning Disabilities* Kidderminster, BILD Publications.

Johnstone, D. (1998) *A Introduction to Disability Studies* London, David Fulton Publishers.

Philpot, T. and Ward, L. (1995) *Values and Visions: Changing ideas in services for people with learning disabilities* London, Butterworth Heinemann.

Simons, K. (1998) *Home, work and inclusion. The social policy implications of supported living and employment for people with learning disabilities*, York, York Publishing Services.

Scottish Executive (2000) *The Same As You? A Review of Services for People with Learning Disabilities*, Edinburgh, Scottish Executive.

Thompson, T. and Mathias, P. (1998) *Standards and Learning Disability* Edinburgh, Harcourt Brace and Co.

Websites

www.arcuk.org.uk ARC (Association of Residential Care), an umbrella organisation of residential providers

www.bild.org.uk Useful information on learning disability, including links to other learning disability organisations

www.bris.ac.uk/Depts/NorahFry A research centre, part of the University of Bristol, with an interest in supporting the rights of people with learning difficulties

www.doh.gov.uk/learningdisabilities Department of Health for England and Wales website

www.doh.gov.uk/london/learningdisabilities contains information of strategic network for London learning disabilities services

www.downs-syndrome.org.uk information on Down's syndrome

www.mencap.org.uk MENCAP provides services for people with learning disabilities

www.ndt.org.uk National Development Team, an independent development agency

www.pwsa-uk.demon.co.uk The Prader Willi Syndrome Association (UK) offers support, advice and advocacy for people with Prader Willi Syndrome, their families and professionals

www.rettsyndrome.org.uk information on Rett Syndrome

www.scotland.gov.uk/ldsr the Scottish Executive site with details of the national review of services for people with learning disabilities in Scotland

www.united-response.co.uk United Response, a provider of housing for people with learning disabilities and mental health problems

www.wales.gov.uk the Welsh Assembly site

Organisations

People First
Central England People First
PO Box 5200
Northampton
NN1 1ZB
Tel: 01604 721666
Website: *www.peoplefirst.org.uk*
Central England People First will be able to give you information on People
First organisations in your area.

City and Guilds Affinity (Awarding body)
1 Giltspur Street
London EC1A9DD
Tel: 0207 294 2800
Email: *enquiry@city-and-guilds.co.uk*
Website: *www.city-and-guilds.co.uk*

Mencap
National Centre
123 Golden Lane
London EC1Y 0RT
Tel: 020 7454 0454
Fax: 020 7608 3254
Email: *information@mencap.org.uk*
Website: *www.mencap.org.uk*

National Open College Network (Awarding body)
University of Derby
Kedleston Road
Derby DE22 1GB
Tel: 01332622712
Email: *nocn@derby.ac.uk*
Website: *www.nocn.ac.uk*

BILD Services

Information Services provides up to date reading lists on over 40 subjects and
literature searches on request. For more information contact 01562 723010.

Learning Services provides in house training, distance learning, conferences
and workshops. The BILD Certificates Programme can provide accreditation
for staff through studying this and other units. For more information contact
01562 723025 email *learning@bild.org.uk*

BILD Publications publishes books, training materials and accessible materials for people with learning disabilities. For a free publications catalogue, and for more information, contact BILD on 01562 723020 email *t.tindell@bild.org.uk*

BILD membership. Discounts on training and publications, a free members' handbook and free subscription to the British Journal of Learning Disabilities. For more information call 01562 723015 or email m.davies@bild.org.uk.

Other titles published by BILD, as part of its programme to support the *Certificates in Working with People who have Learning Disabilities.*

Induction: Starting Work with People with Learning Disabilities
Alice Bradley

A study workbook for staff starting a new job with people with learning disabilities, with clear text and illustrations, and work-based activities.

The workbook provides all the information needed for the Induction – Learning Disability unit of the *Certificate in Working with People who have Learning Disabilities* at Level two, and covers:

- You and your job
- Confidentiality
- About learning disability
- Lessons from history
- Challenging behaviour.

* Does not cover health and safety at work.

2001   ISBN 1 902519 80 9   A4   £12.00

Foundation in Care – Understanding Abuse
Foundation in Care – Understanding Positive Communication
Alice Bradley

Two study workbooks for staff in their first six months of working with people with learning disabilities.

Understanding Abuse covers:

- A disabling society
- Recognising abuse
- Recognising neglect
- Power, control and responsibility.

Understanding Positive Communication covers:

- Communication in more than words
- Communication and physical contact
- Communication and challenging behaviour

- Practical strategies to deal with emotional arousal
- Reports, record-keeping and care plans.

By reading through the workbooks, and carrying out the activities, staff will have all the information they need for the Foundation – Understanding Abuse and Understanding Positive Communication unit of the *Certificate in Working with People who have Learning Disabilities at Level two*.

2001   ISBN 1 902519 89 2   A4   Two units   £20.00

Positive Approaches to Challenging Behaviour (updated and revised)
James Hogg and John Harris

A course of six independent study workbooks for staff and first line managers working with people with learning disabilities who present challenging behaviour.

Topics covered include:

- Understanding the origins of challenging behaviour
- Promoting non-challenging behaviour and responding to people who are emotionally aroused
- Managing challenging behaviour
- Promoting non-challenging behaviour: communication
- Promoting non-challenging behaviour: participation in community life
- Promoting non-challenging behaviour: supporting relationships

The activities throughout the text can be carried out in a variety of care settings, including day and residential services. The workbooks are fully mapped to units from the Level Two and Level Three *Certificates in Working with People who have Learning Disabilities*.

2001   ISBN 1 902519 66 3   A4   £60.00 for the set

To order any of these titles, please contact BILD Publications, Plymbridge Distributors, Estover Road, Plymouth, PL6 7PZ. Tel 01752 202301. Please add 10% for postage and packing.